The
BEANS
& GRAINS
Bible

The
BEANS
& GRAINS
Bible

The ultimate resource: from kidney
beans and black beans to modern
superfoods such as quinoa
and farro

Emma Borghesi

THUNDER BAY
P · R · E · S · S

San Diego, California

Thunder Bay Press
An imprint of Printers Row Publishing Group
10350 Barnes Canyon Road, Suite 100, San Diego CA 92121
www.thunderbaybooks.com

Printers Row Publishing Group is a division of Readerlink Distribution Services, LLC. The Thunder Bay Press name and logo are trademarks of Readerlink Distribution Services, LLC.

All notations of errors or omissions should be addressed to Thunder Bay Press, Editorial Department, at the above address. All other correspondence (author inquiries, permissions) concerning the content of this book should be addressed to Moseley Road, Inc., 129 Main St., Suite B, Irvington, NY 10533.

Thunder Bay Press
Publisher: Peter Norton
Publishing Team: Lori Asbury, Ana Parker, Laura Vignale
Editorial Team: Melinda Allman, Traci Douglas, J. Carroll
Production Team: JoAnn Padgett, Rusty von Dyl

Moseley Road Inc., www.moseleyroad.com
Publisher: Sean Moore
Author, interior design, and layout: Emma Borghesi
Consultant dietitian for meal plans: Danielle Bowman
Cover design: Philippa Baile and Lisa Purcell

Library of Congress Cataloging-in-Publication Data
Borghesi, Emma.
  The beans & grains bible / Emma Borghesi.
     pages cm
  Summary: "Beans and grains have been part of the human diet for centuries. Many stories exist of ancient cultures using these foods not only for sustenance, but also in ritual. The Beans & Grains Bible is a complete source of information on enjoying this naturally nutritious cuisine in your own home. Expert tips on choosing the best produce, storage ideas, and tasty recipes will help you make sure your family gets their daily requirement of these valuable food groups"-- Provided by publisher.
  ISBN 978-1-62686-437-5 (hardback)
1. Cooking (Beans) 2. Cooking (Cereals) 3. Beans--Health aspects. 4.
Vegetarian cooking. I. Title. II. Title: Beans and grains bible.
  TX803.B4B67 2015
  641.6'565--dc23
                          2015018756
Printed in China
19 18 17 16 15 1 2 3 4 5

Warning: To avoid the risk of salmonella, use pasteurized eggs. The pasteurization process kills any harmful bacteria in the egg.

Disclaimer

The information in this book is of a general nature and is intended to help you understand issues concerning nutrition and health; it is not a substitute for professional medical or dietary advice. While all care has been taken in the preparation of its contents, the publisher and the authors accept no liability for damages arising from information in this book. Please always consult your doctor or an accredited dietitian for advice specific to your individual health requirements.

Contents

Author's Note : In this book, the term "bean" refers to the fruit, or part of the fruit (such as the pod or the seed), of a wide range of edible, pod-bearing plants, also known as "legumes." It includes fresh green beans, peas, soybeans, peanuts, lentils, chickpeas, and dry beans (also known as "pulses"), among others.

What's So Great About Beans and Grains?

EVERYONE KNOWS BEANS AND GRAINS ARE HEALTHY,

AND MOST PEOPLE KNOW THEY'RE DELICIOUS, TOO.

BUT WHAT *EXACTLY* IS SO SPECIAL

ABOUT THEM?

IT'S ALL ABOUT THE PROTEIN, ENERGY-GIVING CARBS,

FIBER, FLAVOR, AND SUSTAINABILITY.

The Great Protein Package

What many people don't realize is that mixing beans and grains together in the same meal or eating a variety of beans and grains over the course of a day will provide perfect protein. This dispels the myth that meat-free and low-meat diets are lacking in "complete" protein.

The simple process of pairing one source of protein, such as beans, with another *complementary* protein, such as grains, to provide a complete protein source was once thought to be complicated and time-consuming. Not surprisingly, many people abandoned the idea in a sea of confusion about amino acids. But at least part of this resistance was that it focused on vegetarian food sources at a time when the idea of eating meat as a necessary part of a healthy diet was deeply entrenched.

Conversely, meat-free diets were regarded with suspicion and thought of as lacking in nutrition—so much so that, at times, the scientists researching the benefits of meat-free diets found themselves in the position of needing to understate matters, so as not to upset the food and dietary establishment.

Recently, though, there has been a surge of interest

in vegetarian food. There are so many benefits: vegetarian dishes are nutritious, delicious, affordable, ecologically sustainable, fun to grow and harvest—the list is endless.

Within this more accepting environment, the real truths about the ease and simplicity of a low-meat or meat-free diet are gaining a deserved foothold in our culture. People can easily sustain themselves on such diets—much of the world does already or incorporate some meat-free meals into their lives, without compromising health or nutrition. (More information about complementary protein and the amount of protein needed in the diet can be found on page 25.)

And There's More . . .

The protein benefits are only one part, albeit a large part, of the brilliant beans-and-grains equation. All sorts of other nutritional benefits come into play as well. Beans and grains are both great sources of dietary fiber, so eating them together is an easy way to meet the body's fiber requirements. For the most part, they are also low in fat and excellent sources of

Fast Fact

Beans are the world's most concentrated source of plant-based protein, and they work together with grains to provide a "complete" source of protein.

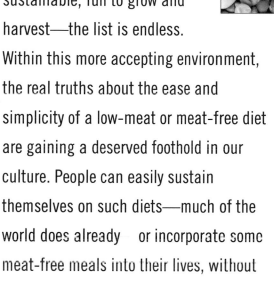

Fast Fact

Beans and grains are great sources of energy-giving carbohydrates and dietary fiber.

low- and medium-GI carbs. And they boast an impressive array of vitamins, minerals, and other plant nutrients (called phytonutrients), such as antioxidants.

Nutrition aside, diets high in beans and grains are sustainable from an ecological and economic point of view. Growing beans and grains is less demanding on the planet than animal-based agriculture; beans even support the planet because of their amazing ability to put essential nitrogen back into the soil and make it available to other plants and animals. Further, beans and grains do not require the same high investment in stock necessary for animal farming, so they can be grown economically from seed up. In this

Fresh salad made with quinoa, corn, avocados, tomatoes, and beans.

way, they also lend themselves to small-scale growing in gardens and communal plots, without the need for special equipment.

High-yielding beans are great plants to grow in a home vegetable garden, but lots of grains can be grown this way, too. So it's not hard to see the economic importance of beans and grains to disadvantaged or isolated communities that have a limited ability to raise animals, or to heavily populated areas where food demands are high. In fact, since ancient times, smaller communities all over the world have been able to sustain themselves through their own homegrown produce and have not had to rely on commercially farmed or grown produce. The driving force for these practices is as simple and primitive as life itself: the need to eat. Meanwhile, contemporary organic farming on both large and small scales reflects renewed interest in these long-held practices, but in this case, the driving forces are primarily sustainability, nutrition, and an increasing demand for organic foods.

Many varieties of beans and grains have evolved sufficiently to enable them to survive in difficult environments—such as harsh, arid climates or cold, steep terrains—and the economic importance of this cannot be understated. Hence, research seeks to establish which grains and beans grow best under which difficult circumstances, with one aim being to develop them further and make them available to communities in need. In the long term, this may provide the answer to famines and dwindling world food supplies.

In this quest, there have been some disappointments along the way, including the development of a wheat hybrid called triticale that was hailed as the answer to food shortages around the world but fell short of its goal (see page 105). However, it is to be expected that the path to success will

be littered with failures, and so the quest continues.

One need not be a vegan or vegetarian to enjoy delicious meals with a focus on beans and grains. Various meats, including beef and chicken, can easily be added to most of the recipes in this book if desired. When meat is added to the recipes, however, smaller quantities will be needed because beans and grains can stretch a meal without altering its flavor or texture significantly. Many times a few mashed beans have been added to burger

Fast Fact

In the late seventeenth century, Queen Elizabeth I enjoyed peas so much that she had them imported to England.

Tending beans in a home garden.

patties, taco filling, and Bolognese sauce with nobody the wiser. Likewise, barley added to broth tends to enhance and enrich it.

So even though bean-and-grain meals are ideal for those who don't eat meat, they are so appetizing that even the most hardened carnivores will soon be consuming—and be consumed by—their delicious flavors and textures. And of course, meals based on bean-and-grain combinations don't have to be the basis of each day's meals. Even including one or two in a weekly diet will reap benefits. Many can also be served as side dishes or starters.

Fast Fact

A breakfast of toast and peanut butter, or a nutty granola or muesli mixed with low-fat milk or soy milk, is a great high-protein way to kick-start your day.

Facing page: Mexican food with refried beans, an enchilada, and rice.

Below: Muesli made with peanuts, oats, dried fruit, and seeds.

Beans, Grains, and Nutrition

What Does It All Mean?

To appreciate the benefits of beans and grains, and of a healthy diet in general, a basic understanding of nutrition is needed. Included here is a short introduction, but a wealth of additional information is readily available in books and on the Internet. When researching information from the Internet, be sure to use credible sources such as universities, health authorities, and accredited nutritional organizations and databases to ensure the reliability of the information.

No food can offer miracle cures or provide a fountain of youth. Still, food nutrients play a major role in helping to stave off and even prevent certain health- and age-related disorders because, in addition to providing energy, they help support and maintain the body and all its functions. Nutrients also have a role in the body's repair and detoxification processes. At the same time, care needs to be taken with *anti-nutrients*, those compounds found in food that are detrimental rather than beneficial to the body. A meal comprised mainly of beans and grains eaten once or twice a week, for instance, won't fix the problems caused by too much fat, sugar, alcohol, and processed foods, which

Peanut butter, whole-grain bread, and bananas.

will sabotage the efforts of even the most diligent healthy foods. Given a chance, however, beans and grains will show just how health-boosting they can be.

What Are Nutrients?

Nutrients are the compounds found in food that enable the body to grow and function. Once in the body, they facilitate all the chemical reactions that allow us to develop, grow, mature, maintain, repair, react, think, sleep, be active . . . and everything in between.

The term "essential nutrients" refers to seven types of nutrients that are essential for life. They are as follows:

- Vitamins
- Minerals
- Carbohydrates
- Proteins
- Fats
- Dietary Fiber
- Water

The first five are absorbed into the body and have specific roles to play. Of these, carbohydrates, proteins, and fats are known as macronutrients because they exist in a tangible form and because they need to be eaten in significant quantities. Vitamins and minerals, on the other hand, are known as micronutrients because they can be seen only on a microscopic scale within other foods and because they are consumed in small, yet effective, quantities.

The sixth nutrient, dietary fiber, is not generally digested, so some nutritionists, while acknowledging its importance, do not classify it as a nutrient. In this book, however, given its high profile in beans and grains, dietary fiber is regarded as an essential nutrient.

The seventh nutrient is water. The largest component of our bodies, water exists in every cell, and is needed in some way or another in all bodily functions, from the invisible chemical reactions that take place all the time within us to thermoregulation (maintaining the body's temperature), transportation of fluids, and excretion.

Although beans and grains offer many essential nutrients, they are

Tofu made from soybeans.

Fast Fact

Powerful phytonutrients,
including antioxidants, are
found in the seeds and pods
of beans, and also
in the bran of grains.

especially important as sources of plant-based protein, and therefore are major components of vegetarian and vegan diets. They are also major contributors of low- and medium-GI carbohydrates and dietary fiber. It is important to remember that while foods are commonly called a carbohydrate, a protein, or a fat, most contain a combination of some or all of the seven nutrients in various quantities and ratios. Therefore, when a piece of chicken is referred to as a protein, this means only that protein is the macronutrient in greatest proportion overall. The chicken also contains some fat and various micronutrients. Similarly, a nut might be called a fat, but it contains protein and carbs in smaller proportions.

Another group of micronutrients are called phytonutrients and are found in plants. Like vitamins and minerals, they are active compounds that play a role in helping to slow the aging process, and guard against certain cancers and cardiovascular diseases. These phytonutrients include powerful antioxidants found in the color pigments of plants (carotene, for example). Other phytonutrients occur in the bran layer of grains or in the thin skin surrounding seeds, called the seed coat. This is one of the reasons, along with fiber content and various others, that whole grains are considered healthier than refined grains.

Although there appear to be thousands of phytonutrients in plants, there is still relatively little conclusive research on their number, how they work on their own, and how they interact with other compounds. For these reasons, they are not yet recognized as "essential nutrients." However, indications are that the health implications are far-reaching and positive. A guide to some of the most commonly known phytonutrients can be found on page 45.

With the exception of soybeans, peanuts, and (to a lesser extent) lupinis, grains and beans are also low in fat—and the fat that they do have is the "good," polyunsaturated type. They also contain some plant sterols, compounds in plants that can help lower blood cholesterol, a known risk factor for cardiovascular diseases.

A classic, simple meal: baked beans in tomato sauce.

What Do the Essential Nutrients Do?

Each type of nutrient has its own role in the body. The three macronutrients can be thought of as follows:

Protein gives the body, and every cell in it, a physical form and structure. If the body were a building, protein would be its bricks and all its internal components, both large and small.

Carbohydrates give the body energy. If the body were a car, the carbohydrates would be the gas. And, just like gas, the quality of carbohydrates varies.

Fats pad the body, help keep it warm, and act as a reserve food source if the carbs run out. If the body were a chair, the fat would be the stuffing—but in times of need, the stuffing would be taken out and used for fuel!

The two types of essential micronutrients are vitamins and minerals:

Vitamins and minerals play an important part in the various chemical processes that take place in the body all the time. Minerals also help provide structure, such as the calcium found in bones. The nutrition tables (see page 36) provide further information about the main vitamins and minerals and their roles in the body.

Tending a rice paddy in China.

Fiber helps push food through the digestive system so the nutrients in those foods can be absorbed and waste can be eliminated. There are three types: soluble fiber, insoluble fiber, and resistant starch.

Water is the largest physical component of our bodies. It is present in every cell and is needed for every bodily process and function.

Beans, Grains, and Their Protein, Carbs, and Fiber

When it comes to beans and grains, these three essential macronutrients are of special importance.

Protein

Protein might form our bodies' "building blocks," but what are the building blocks themselves, and why are they so important? Proteins are made up of smaller, microscopic proteins known as amino acids. When protein is consumed, the digestive system breaks it down into amino acids that then rebuild in different configurations to form the physical components of our bodies. So each piece of protein we eat, whether it is a bean or a piece of meat, is used to build and repair parts of the body itself.

Fast Fact

One cup of beans and two slices of bread has as much protein as a 3-oz. serving of meat.

Green bean casserole made with fresh beans, mushrooms, onions, and rice.

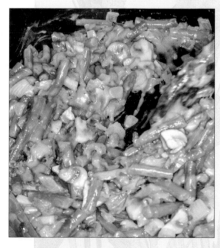

Quinoa and chickpea salad.

Fast Fact

Although grains are thought of as carbohydrates, they are also between 7 and 15 percent protein, and are the main source of protein in some countries.

Protein, Amino Acids, and Meat-Free Diets

The big issue surrounding protein and meat-free diets is all about amino acids. There are nineteen standard amino acids that an adult human body needs for growth and functioning. Fortunately, a healthy human body makes eleven of these for itself. They are called "nonessential" amino acids because they are not an essential part of your diet (since your body makes them). Some of these nonessential amino acids, however, may be hard for the body to make when it is sick or under significant stress, which is one reason it is important to stay healthy and avoid stress as much as possible.

The remaining eight amino acids are called "essential" because it is essential that the body source them from food.

Here is the tricky part: animal proteins contain all eight essential amino acids. As a result, the protein found in meats is considered to be a complete protein. Most plant-based proteins, on the other hand, do not contain all eight. Therefore, we cannot obtain all the amino acids we need if our only protein source is beans. For this reason, most plant-based proteins are referred to as incomplete or limited proteins. This is not to suggest they are of poor quality—in fact, many plant foods are excellent sources of protein. Rather, it means that they do not contain a complete set of all the essential amino acids, so the missing ones need to be sourced from other foods.

What Are Complementary Proteins?

Fortunately, the essential amino acids missing from one plant food can be found in another. Foods that work together in this way are known as complementary proteins. Beans, especially dry beans combined with grains, are the perfect example. And when it comes to beans and grains, you don't need to be able to list all the amino acids or even know which ones are essential. Nor do you need to know how much of each needs to be eaten. All you need to know is that most grains do not have, or have insufficient quantities of, just one amino acid, lysine. Dry beans, however, have loads of lysine, so if you eat a meal of grains mixed with beans, your protein needs for that meal are met.

A Lebanese feast: hummus, tabbouleh, kibbeh, falafel, and pita bread.

Some recent research suggests that the beans and grains don't even have to be eaten in the same meal. Rather, as long as a variety of proteins are eaten in the same day, the body will find what amino acids it needs and use them.

That said, some beans and grains work so well in meal combinations, compatible in both flavor and nutrition, that there appears to be no need to spread them over different meals. A moment's thought will bring to mind all sorts of popular bean-and-grain combinations: tacos and other Mexican dishes with refried beans, pesto pasta mixed with green beans, soups with beans and barley, sandwiches with bean sprouts, salads with sprouts and cracked wheat, stir-fries with noodles or rice, and baked beans on toast, to mention just a few.

With some exceptions, most beans are also lacking in one essential amino acid (methionine). But just as beans give lysine to grains, grains supply the methionine and any other amino acids of which there might be a shortfall. In that way, bean-and-grain combinations make one complete protein source.

It can be helpful to know a little bit about amino acids, but not if it becomes a source of worry and prevents you from trusting beans and grains in combination as a reliable source of protein. A much better idea is to include servings of both beans and grains in your

Other Great Combinations

Beans with Seeds and Nuts: Seeds from sunflowers and sesames, and nuts such as almonds, walnuts, pistachios, and pecans, make another great pairing with beans (be mindful, though, that tree nuts are a major food allergen—see page 163). So nutty trail mixes that include seeds (perhaps even some carob pieces), falafels served with tahini (sesame paste), and hummus made from chickpeas and tahini are all great combinations and ideal for snacks or quick meals.

Grains with Seeds and Nuts: Nuts and seeds also complement grains, so oatmeal with nuts or seeds sprinkled on top, or almond butter on toast, are both good sources of complete protein.

daily diet and to include at least one with each meal. It may be that with time you will become so excited and inspired by vegetarian food that you will begin to research it more thoroughly and become something of an expert on proteins and amino acids. If not, and if you just want to eat your food and enjoy it and stay healthy at the same time, that's perfectly fine. Just make sure that if you eat only plant foods, you include a variety of grains and beans in your diet each day.

Of note: some plant foods, such as soy and quinoa, do provide all the amino acids and don't need to be paired with other foods to fill any gaps. Therefore, adding things such as tofu, tempeh, soy milk, and quinoa into your weekly diet will give a nice protein boost; likewise with dairy foods, such as yogurt, milk, cheese, and eggs. Nuts and seeds also pair well with beans in the same way grains do, so you can use them to make great protein-boosting snacks.

A varied diet of whole foods is the best way to ensure that our bodies get all the nutrients they need—not just protein, but carbs, fats,

Fast Fact

Most people need only 0.36 gram of protein per pound of body weight (or 0.8 gram per kilogram) per day.

Middle Eastern chickpea and barley soup.

Fast Fact

Alfalfa sprouts and
beanshoots are both
types of bean sprouts.

vitamins, minerals, fiber, and water. Beans and grains are part of that healthy mix. And don't forget that a few delicious surprises, such as alfalfa sprouts, beanshoots, peanuts, carob, and even the maize in tortillas—are all just waiting to be mixed together into lots of tasty, nutritious combinations.

How Much Protein Do We Need?

Many of us worry too much about how much protein we are getting, and in turn worry unnecessarily about the adequacy of protein in vegetarian and vegan diets. To put our minds at rest, it is worth knowing that the U.S. recommended daily allowance (RDA) of protein for most moderately active adults is only 0.36 gram of protein per pound of body weight per day. For

Hummus and falafel.

example, if you weigh 140 pounds, and in the absence of any particular demands for a higher-than-usual intake, your daily protein requirement will be around only 51 grams.

Just one cup of beans per day (excluding fresh green beans and peas, which have lower protein levels) provides about 15 grams of protein, compared to about 21 grams offered by a 3-ounce serving of meat. Two slices of whole-grain bread supplies another 6 grams of protein. Hence, one cup of beans and two slices of bread offers about the same amount of protein as 3 ounces of meat. Add in a 3-ounce serving of tofu (an additional 13 grams), and you're already two-thirds of the way to your daily target. Nuts, nut butters, and seeds are also great sources of protein, as are all dairy foods. Even vegetables make valuable contributions. So it's easy to get all the protein you need from non-meat sources. If you want more information on the protein component of foods, the nutrition labels on the grains and dry beans will provide this, and more is readily available from reputable sources on the Internet. Keep in mind, too, that while all cereal grains offer some protein, wheat and oats have the highest amounts, followed by rye and barley, and then millet, rice, and corn.

In general, people on vegetarian and vegan diets tend to weigh less than meat-eaters, which means their daily requirements for protein are also a little less. And since it is healthier to maintain a lower body weight, many people find that to be more achievable with a diet that is partially or completely meat-free.

There is no need to give up meat altogether, but many nutritionists believe that the greatest focus should be placed on fresh vegetables and grains, with less emphasis on animal protein. Good-quality dairy foods and meat are nutritious, of course, but a little goes a long way and it is possible that many of us are eating more of those foods than we need.

With all this in mind, it becomes clear that vegetarians and vegans don't need to eat copious quantites of plant-based protein to meet their dietary needs. As long as beans, grains, and a varied diet are in the equation, most people's protein needs can be met easily. Ideally, protein should be included with every meal so that intake is

spread over the day. This is especially so in the case of vegan and vegetarian diets.

All that said, some people—especially athletes, or those who have physically strenuous jobs or certain health conditions—may have higher requirements for protein (and other nutrients). So, no matter the diet, don't make sudden and dramatic changes without first consulting a medical practitioner or a qualified dietician regarding your individual requirements, especially if you have any particular health issues or concerns.

Carbohydrates

Healthy carbohydrates include fruits, vegetables, grains, and beans. Less

Fast Fact

Many bean plants are used as green manure. They are turned back into the soil at the end of the season, when they break down and release nitrogen.

Fast Fact

nutritious types are table sugar and refined white flour. Beans and grains are both excellent sources of healthy carbohydrates and most have a low to medium GI (glycemic index). This means they break down more slowly than high-GI carbs. The benefit of low-GI carbs is that they release energy at a slower and more sustained rate than high-GI foods. This is important to blood-sugar levels because it helps avoid the sudden peaks, troughs, and associated problems with insulin levels, hunger, and mood. Low-GI carbs, therefore, help to treat and prevent conditions such as diabetes and hypoglycemia. And from a weight-management perspective, they help to control appetite, promote satiety, and curb hunger. Information on the GI levels of several beans and grains can be found on page 47.

Dietary Fiber

There are three types of fiber: soluble fiber, insoluble fiber, and resistant starch. While the benefits of soluble fiber and insoluble fiber have been known for quite some time,

it is only recently that a greater understanding of resistant starch has come to light.

Soluble fiber dissolves in water and forms a gel-like substance that helps make us feel full. It can also help remove harmful LDL cholesterol, which contributes to cardiovascular conditions. Various cooked whole grains contain modest amounts of soluble fiber, and oats and beans are excellent sources.

Insoluble fiber helps speed food through the bowel. This is important because it helps to limit the amount of time that toxic substances are in contact with the lining of the bowel, a factor that can contribute to various disorders. Insoluble fiber also reduces the risk of developing constipation, colitis, bowel cancer, and hemorrhoids. Beans and whole grains are great sources of insoluble fiber.

Resistant starch is a newcomer to the sphere of nutritional knowledge. It is a type of fiber that passes through the digestive system until it reaches the

Fast Fact

People who eat six or more servings of grains per day have a reduced risk of type 2 diabetes, heart disease, stroke, high blood pressure, and certain cancers.

33

Fast Fact

large intestine, where it breaks down and produces compounds that may help protect against bowel cancer. It also helps to reduce insulin resistance and to lower blood sugar, while increasing feelings of fullness and satiety. Beans and most whole grains are good sources of resistant starch. Interestingly, cold, cooked starchy foods, such as rice, potatoes, and pasta are also great sources. It was originally thought that the resistant starch in these cold foods was lost upon reheating, but recent research suggests that in many cases most of the resistant starch appears to be retained.

Facing page: Pasta and bean salad.

Grains and Beans: Best Features

So, what are the main benefits of beans and grains?

- When combined, they provide an easy and complete source of plant-based protein.
- They are good sources of energy-giving carbohydrates.
- They provide plenty of fiber.
- They provide various vitamins, minerals, and phytonutrients.
- They are delicious.
- They offer affordable and sustainable food sources that can be grown on a large or small scale.

Nutrition Tables

The first three tables on the following pages are intended as guides to the micronutrients that can be found in both beans and grains. Keep in mind that available amounts may vary, depending on factors such as local climate, soil conditions, and how fresh the produce is, but the tables offer a useful starting point. Other sources of the various nutrients are also provided.

The fourth table provides information on the known GI values of various beans and grains. Here again, there will be variations between foods of the same type, so these can be used only as a guide. In assessing the GI levels of specific foods, it is easier to think of them in terms of low-GI, medium-GI, and high-GI. For the most part, favor low- and medium-GI foods over high-GI foods.

Vitamins

Vitamins are needed in minute quantities in the body to ensure its proper functioning. They are classified into two groups: water soluble and fat soluble.

Water-soluble vitamins—the B vitamins and vitamin C— dissolve in the body's fluids, and excesses are excreted in urine. Water-soluble vitamins must be replenished to prevent deficiencies.

The fat-soluble vitamins are A, D, E, and K. Unlike their water-soluble cousins, excess amounts are stored in the body rather than excreted, meaning the body can draw on these stores when they are needed. There is, however, a limit to how much of each fat-soluble vitamin the body is able to store, and excesses building up over time can result in unpleasant side effects, so they should not be consumed in excess.

Vitamin deficiencies are common, where the body has neither sufficient amounts for immediate use nor, in the case of fat-soluble vitamins, reserves to draw on. Vitamin D, for example, is largely dependent on exposure to sunlight, but an increased tendency for people to protect their skin from sun exposure combined with more time spent indoors has contributed to worldwide vitamin D deficiences—even in sunny climates. Long winters with little sunshine can also lead to vitamin D deficiencies.

The following tables outline some important vitamins.

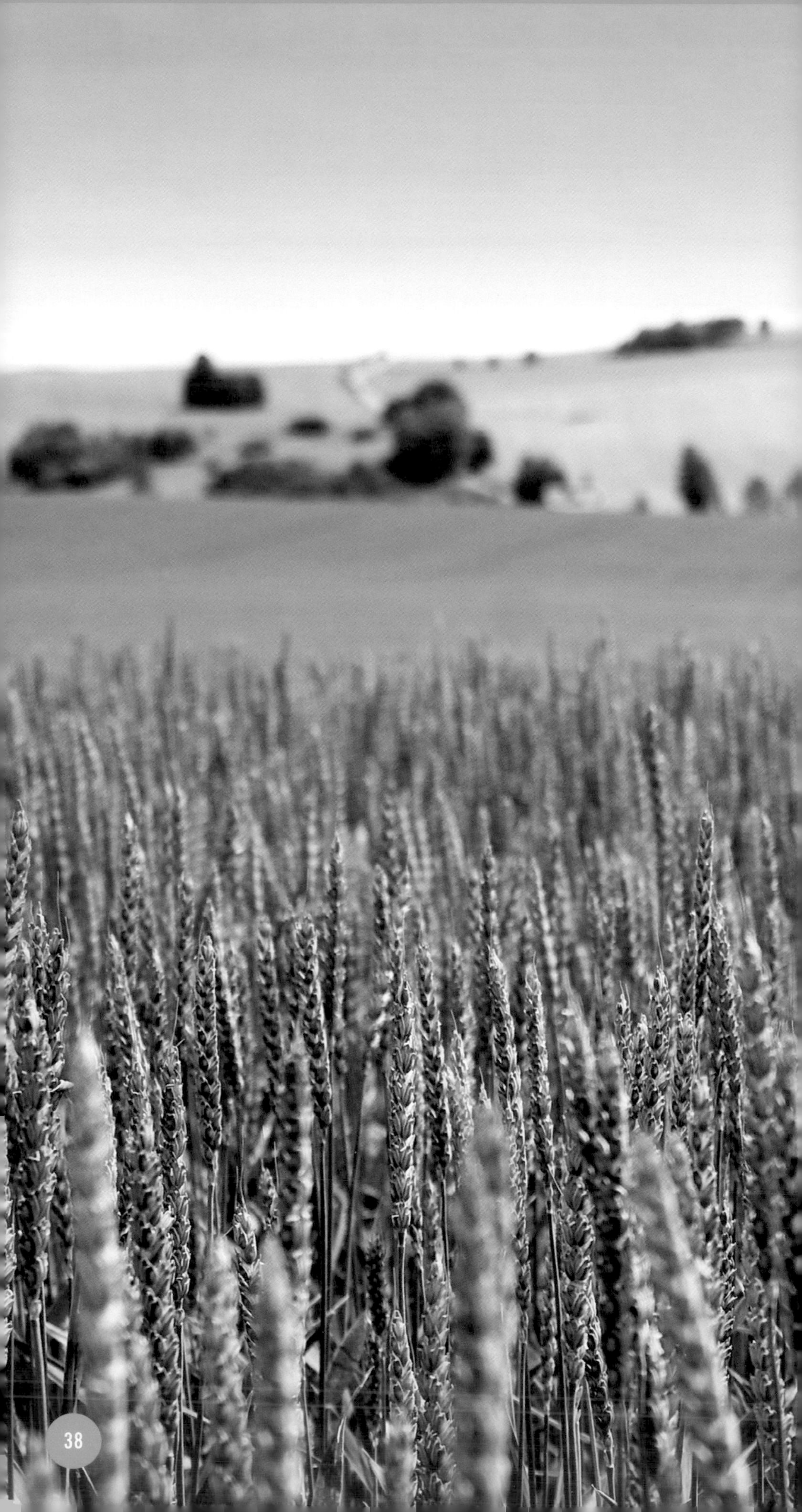

Vitamin A

Vitamin A is found in plant foods in the form of carotenoids, the pigments that give carrots and other red, orange, and yellow plant foods their colors. The human body converts some of the carotenoids into vitamin A. Carotenoids are powerful antioxidants, and of the 500 or more found in nature, the most studied have been beta-carotene, lycopene, zeaxanthin, and beta-cryptoxanthin. Research suggests that these antioxidants may help strengthen the immune system and reduce risk of certain cancers and heart disease.

Vitamin A is needed for	
• healthy eyesight, skin, and mucus membranes. • immunity and growth.	• Beans and grains are **not** significant sources of vitamin A. Some provide none. • Good plant sources include bell peppers, carrots, mangoes, canteloupe, romaine lettuce, and sweet potatoes.

B Vitamins

These water-soluble vitamins are especially important for enabling the body to produce energy, and for keeping the skin, nervous system, and digestive system healthy. They include vitamins B1, B2, B3, B5, B6, B7, B9, B12, and others. The somewhat confusing omission of some numbers in the naming system is the result of later renaming or reclassification. Some are called by their other names—for example, vitamin B9 is folic acic. And some, such as vitamin B15 (pangamic acid), arc not significant enough to include here.

B1 (thiamine)	
• metabolizes carbohydrates and releases energy. • aids appetite and digestion. • supports heart and nervous system.	• Good plant sources include chia seeds, beans, oats, millet, and sorghum. • Other plant sources include nuts (macadamia, pistachio, Brazil, pecan, cashew), seeds (sesame, sunflower, pumpkin), and squash.
B2 (riboflavin) helps to	
• maintain healthy skin and eyes. • metabolize carbohydrates, proteins, and fats; and release energy. • support nervous and digestive systems.	• Good plant sources include chia seeds, pigeon peas, and chestnuts. • Other good sources include other seeds, nuts, mushrooms, spinach, and collard greens.
B3 (niacin)	
• helps to metabolize carbohydrates, alcohol, and fat, and to release energy. • is essential for growth, and healthy hair, skin, eyes, liver, and nervous system.	• Good plant sources include whole grains and beans. • Other good sources include nuts, mushrooms, passion fruit, and avocados.
B5 (pantothenic acid) helps to	
• metabolize carbohydrates, protein, fat, and alcohol to release energy. • prevent anemia by assisting in the formation of red blood cells. • produce steroid hormones.	• Good plant sources include beans and peanuts.

B6 (pyridoxine) assists in • protein and carbohydrate metabolism. • the formation of red blood cells and prevention of anemia. • the production of brain chemicals. • immune function and steroid hormone activity.	• Good plant sources include rice, peas, and nuts • Grains contain modest amounts. • Other good sources include leafy green vegetables and bananas.
B7 (biotin) is needed for • energy production. • glycogen synthesis.	• Good plant sources include peanuts and oats. • Other good sources include cauliflower, mushrooms, tomatoes, carrots, and walnuts.
B9 (folate) assists in the • prevention of neural tube defects. • metabolism of DNA. • prevention of anemia. • formation of enzymes and red blood cells. • control of levels of homocysteine, a chemical in the blood that is associated with heart attacks, strokes, and blood clots when elevated.	• Good plant sources include leafy green vegetables, beans, whole grains, and seeds. • Other good sources include citrus fruits.
B12 (cobalamin) assists in • metabolism. • the functioning of the nervous system. • the prevention of pernicious anemia. • the formation of blood cells. • controlling levels of homocysteine, a chemical in the blood that is associated with heart attacks, strokes, and blood clots when elevated.	• Vitamin B12 is not found in significant quantities in plant food. Best sources for vegetarians include yogurt, fortified almond milk, fortified coconut milk, dairy milk, and eggs.

Vitamin C

This water-soluble vitamin is a powerful antioxidant. It has long been used to prevent the onset of colds and flu, but recent research suggests it may reduce the duration of such illnesses rather than prevent them. Perhaps of most interest is its role in helping to prevent certain cancers. Low levels of vitamin C appear to be associated with an increased risk of various cancers, particularly those of the mouth, stomach, esophagus, pancreas, and cervix. Deficiencies also cause scurvy.

Vitamin C supports • natural immunity. • healthy gums, teeth, and bones. • healing wounds. • iron absorption.	• Lima beans provide some vitamin C. • Other plant sources include bell peppers, leafy green vegetables, kiwifruit, broccoli, berries, citrus fruits, papaya, and melons.

Vitamin D

Vitamin D is a fat-soluble vitamin that is produced by the body through exposure to sunlight. It is not possible to source adequate vitamin D from food, so many people take vitamin D supplements, especially during the winter. Low vitamin D levels appear to be linked to several diseases, though it is not clear whether deficiencies arise as a result of specific diseases, or vice versa. In particular, its possible roles in preventing certain cancers, boosting the immune system, and treating and preventing depression are the subject of ongoing research.

Vitamin D	
Vitamin D • assists in bone formation. • boosts the absorption of calcium and phosphorus. • helps guard against osteoporosis and rickets.	• Vitamin D is produced by the skin after exposure to the UV rays in sunlight. However, small amounts are found in some foods, such as fortified milk or cereal.

Vitamin E

Vitamin E is a fat-soluble vitamin and an antioxidant that is being researched for its possible role in preventing cancer and heart disease. Vitamin E has also long been used in topical treatments to assist in healing wounds and the treatment of scars, but as yet there is no definitive scientific evidence in support of these claims.

Vitamin E	
Vitamin E • supports the immune system. • is a powerful antioxidant. • is undergoing continuing research regarding its possible role in helping to prevent cancer and heart disease.	• Oats provide some vitamin E. The germ (or seed embryo) in whole grains also contains vitamin E, but that is lost in refined grains. • Nuts and seeds are also good sources of vitamin E. • Other sources include avocados and olive oil.

Vitamin K

Vitamin K is a fat-soluble vitamin. It is produced in the body by intestinal bacteria and is also found in some foods.

Vitamin K	
Vitamin K • assists in helping the blood to clot.	• Good plant sources of vitamin K include herbs (parsley, basil, chives, watercress), leafy green vegetables (spinach, collard greens, broccoli rabe), romaine lettuce, celery, cucumbers, broccoli, fennel, and prunes.

Minerals

Minerals are essential for regulating the body's water balance and enabling its chemical reactions. They also form the hard structures such as bones and teeth. Fourteen of the most important minerals are described below.

Calcium	
Calcium assists in • bone formation and strength. • nerve and muscle function. • blood pressure control. • weight control.	• Good plant sources include amaranth, soy products, nuts, and seeds. • Other good sources include milk, yogurt, cheese, leafy green vegetables, fortified breads, and fruit juices.
Chromium	
Chromium • is important for normal growth. • assists the action of insulin. • helps to control blood glucose levels.	• Good plant sources include barley, oats, and green beans. • Other good sources include broccoli, tomatoes, and black pepper.
Copper	
Copper • is an important component of enzymes. • has a role in red blood cell production and nervous system function.	• Good plant sources of copper include kale, mushrooms, sesame seeds, nuts, prunes, and avocados.
Fluoride	
Fluoride • is important for strong bones and teeth. • protects against tooth decay. • may protect against osteoporosis.	• Green beans provide some fluoride. • The main source is fluoridated water. • Other sources include celery and radishes.
Iodine	
Iodine is needed for • thyroid function. • energy metabolism.	• Green beans provide some iodine. • Best sources are iodized salt and seaweed. Other sources include bananas and strawberries.
Iron	
Iron • helps form hemoglobin. • prevents anemia. • assists cognitive function and motor development. • boosts immunity.	• Good plant sources include whole grains, beans, nuts, and seeds. • Other good sources include cacao and dried fruit.

Magnesium

Magnesium is needed for • growth and bone health. • the functioning of nerves, muscles, and many other parts of the body. • neutralizing stomach acid and moving stools through the intestines.	• Good plant sources include whole grains, dark leafy green vegetables, and avocados.

Manganese

Manganese is needed for • enzyme activation.	• Good plant sources include whole grains, nuts, and seeds. • Other good plant sources include dark leafy green vegetables (especially kale and spinach).

Molybdenum

Molybdenum • contributes to use of iron in the body. • assists in the metabolism of waste.	• Good plant sources include beans and whole grains. • Other good sources include tomatoes.

Phosphorus

Phosphorus is important for • the formation of bones and teeth. • the body's use of carbohydrates and fats. • the growth, maintenance, and repair of cells and body tissues. • storing energy. • kidney function. • maintaining a normal heartbeat. • proper nerve signaling. • muscle contractions.	• Good plant sources of phosphorus include seeds (chia, sesame, pumpkin) and lentils. • Low fat dairy products are also a good source.

Potassium

Potassium helps • muscles to contract. • to maintain fluid balance in the body and a normal blood pressure. • to maintain a regular heartbeat.	• Good plant sources include cannellini beans, peanuts, lentils, tepary beans, adzukis, pigeon peas, yardlong beans, and amaranth. • Other good sources include dark leafy green vegetables, dried apricots, mushrooms, bananas, and avocados.

Selenium	
Selenium • has an important role in metabolism.	• Good plant sources include lima beans, chia seeds, Brazil nuts, flaxseed, broccoli, cabbage, and spinach.
Sodium	
Sodium • is used by the body to control blood pressure and blood volume. • helps muscles and nerves to function properly.	• Good plant sources of sodium include the tropical mammee apple, guavas, passion fruit, celery root, artichokes, beets, carrots, and celery.
Zinc	
Zinc • is needed for the body's immune system to work properly. • plays a role in cell division, growth, and healing wounds. • helps to metabolize carbohydrates. • is needed for smell and taste.	• Good plant sources of zinc include beans, spinach, pumpkin seeds, and cacao.

Pasta and fresh salad makes a nutritious meal.

Phytonutrients

These plant nutrients appear to help slow the aging process, offer some protection against cardiovascular conditions, and reduce the risk and development of some cancers, among other things. There is, however, much still to be learned. Phytonutrients include antioxidants that neutralize damaging compounds in the body known as free radicals. Some vitamins—A, C, and E—are also considered antioxidants and have undergone the most research to date. A short summary of some of the known information is detailed below.

Isoflavones	
• Major sources include beans, especially soy and soy products. • Rye and flaxseed are also good sources.	• These may help prevent the onset of osteoporosis and reduce the risk of breast cancer. • The estrogen-like qualities of phytoestrogen, an isoflavone found in soy, may help ease the symptoms of menopause.
Lignans	
• Lignans are found whole grains and beans, as well as flaxseeds, bran, fruits, and vegetables.	• Lignans appear to offer similar benefits to isoflavones.
Saponins	
• Good sources include quinoa, oats, and beans, including soybeans, chickpeas, lentils, and alfalfa sprouts.	• Saponins may help slow the rate of cancer growth.
Phytates	
• Beans, whole grains, and bran are rich sources of phytates.	• Phytates are thought to have anticancer properties.
Courmarins	
• These are found in whole grains and bran, as well as in some vegetables and citrus fruit.	• Courmarins may help combat or reduce the growth of certain cancers.

Carotenoids

- These are the orange, yellow, and red pigments found in orange, yellow, and red produce such as pumpkin, carrots, oranges, and tomatoes.
- They are also found in green produce, including green beans, although the colors are masked by cholorophyll.

- Carotenoids are antioxidants that help protect against cancer.
- Carotenoids support immune function.
- Lycopene, a type found in tomatoes, decreases the risk of prostate cancer.
- Two others, lutein and zeaxanthin, help preserve eyesight.

Flavonoids

- Good sources of flavonoids include tea, wine, grapes, onions, berries, and apples. They appear in smaller amounts in other green fruits and vegetables, including fresh beans.

- These antixodants help reduce oxidization of bad LDL cholesterol, which increases the risk of atherosclerosis, stroke, and heart disease.

Catechins

- These are found in green and black tea.

- They may protect against heart disease and some cancers.

Anthocyanins

- These are the blue-purple pigments in produce such as blueberries and beets.

- These antixodants have antibacterial properties.

Indoles and isothiocyanates

- These are found in cruciferous produce such as cabbage and broccoli.

- They may help inhibit the development of certain cancers.

Allicin and other sulfur compounds

- These compounds are found in plant foods such as garlic, onions, leeks, and chives.

- These help thin the blood.
- They have antibacterial properties.
- They help activate growth and repair.

Terpenes

- These are found mainly in citrus fruit.

- These are thought to reduce the risk of breast and skin cancers.

Curcumin

- This is found in spices such as turmeric and mustard.

- These help reduce inflammation.
- They may help prevent cancer.

Ellagic acid

- Ellagic acid is found in grapes, strawberries, and raspberries.

- Ellagic acid may help inhibit carcinogens.

Glycemic Index

The glycemic index (GI) describes the impact of foods on blood sugar, with a low GI (L) being within the range of 55 or less; a medium GI (M) between 55 and 70; and a high GI (H) at 70 or above. Low-GI foods are slower to digest and result in a slower and more sustained release of energy, which also keeps blood sugar levels stable. This has far-reaching implications for the management of weight and blood-sugar disorders such as diabetes, and for a person's mood. Low-GI foods are also more satisfying than high-GI foods, and they are generally high in fiber and low in refined carbohydrates, including sugar.

Whole grains are an excellent source of carbohydrates with low to medium GIs, whereas refined grains generally have higher GIs. Whole-grain flours have a medium GI, but the GI of refined flours and thickeners made from non-grain sources such as potatoes, arrowroot, tapioca, and semolina tend to be in the higher range.

Beans (pods and seeds) are all low-GI.

Whole grains		Ancient grains	
Barley	M	Einkorn	L
Maize (corn)	M	Emmer	L
Millet	M	Spelt	L
Oats	M	Khorasan	L
Rice	M–H*	**Pseudograins**	
Rye	L	Amaranth seeds	L
Sorghum	M	Buckwheat	L
Wheat	M	Kañiwa	L
Triticale	M	Quinoa	L

* Long-grain rices such as basmati rice have a medium GI, but short-grain rices generally have a high GI.

Going with the
Grains

Sometimes called the "seeds of civilization," grains have been the main food staple of the human race since earliest times. Prehistoric nomads gathered the grains they needed to sustain and nourish themselves, moving on to greener pastures when the seasons changed or supplies ran out. Around 12,000 years ago, humans began to acquire the skills to cultivate grains, and then to harvest and store them for longer periods. This led to many people settling in one place, growing crops, and grazing animals on nearby land. From these small communities, the great civilizations of the world emerged. This period marks a transition in many cultures from hunter-gatherer tribes to settled farming communities and is generally called the early Neolithic period (around 10,000–2000 BC), or the period of the first agricultural revolution.

The history of grains, the human race, geographic discoveries around the globe, and the cultural migration of people and foods are all linked. Many grains, in particular barley and ancient wheats, were first cultivated some 10,000 years ago in what is known as the Fertile Crescent, a crescent-shaped stretch of land in the present-day Middle East just east of the Mediterranean Sea. Later, people in other regions learned to farm their own crops from the grains found in their areas. For example, rye was first cultivated in Europe some 9,000 years ago, and maize in the Americas approximately 5,000 years ago. And so, wheat and barley sustained the ancient Egyptians, and later the people of ancient Greece and Rome; maize (corn) fed the Aztecs and Incas of the Americas; and rice has always been the staple food of Asia. Oats and rye were favored by people of the colder, northern reaches of Europe; millet was the food of Africa and various parts of Asia. In Australia, where grains such as wheat were not introduced until after British colonization, indigenous people fed on bushfoods and wildlife.

For many centuries, some grains did not find their way to the Americas from Europe, Asia, and Africa or vice versa because people had no way of dispersing them across such expansive geographic areas—and of course, for the most part, the people of these times had no knowledge of each others' existence. It wasn't until explorer Christopher Columbus traveled the globe in the late 1400s and came upon the previously unknown Americas that the cross-continental spread of grains began. European seeds were introduced to the Americas, and others (largely of South American origin) were brought back to Europe.

Christopher Columbus (c. 1451–1506)

Born in Genoa, Italy, Christopher Columbus was a sailor almost his entire life. After various expeditions in the Atlantic Ocean and to Africa, he conducted an expedition westward from Europe in 1492 with the support of King Ferdinand of Spain. Columbus's goal was to find an alternative trade route from Europe to India and China. Such a route had not been explored before, but Columbus believed it would be quicker and safer than making the trip east overland through unfriendly regions.

After more than a month at sea, Columbus stumbled on the Americas, the existence of which was previously unknown to Europeans. He arrived in what is today the Bahamas, claimed it for Spain, and then ventured further into the vast continent.

Columbus's expedition opened up the Americas, called the New World, to European colonization. The effort became known

as the Columbian Exchange, and it initiated the first migration of people, cultures, plants, animals, and diseases between the European and American continents, with profound and enduring global implications.

Posthumous portrait of Columbus
By Sebastiano del Piombo

What Makes a Serving?

According to the Whole Grains Council, and based on the 2010 Dietary Guidelines for the United States, a whole-grain serving is equal to the following:

- ½ cup cooked brown rice or other cooked grain
- ½ cup cooked 100 percent whole-grain pasta
- ½ cup cooked hot cereal, such as oatmeal
- 1 ounce of uncooked whole-grain pasta, brown rice, or other grain
- 1 slice of 100-percent whole-grain bread
- 1 small (1 ounce) whole-grain muffin
- 1 cup 100-percent whole-grain, ready-to-eat cereal

For other foods that aren't included in the Dietary Guidelines and for foods that contain a mix of whole-grain and refined ingredients, the only way to determine whether they constitute a full serving of whole grains is by looking at the different proportions of the various ingredients. One whole-grain serving is equal to a total of 16 grams of whole-grain ingredients. Therefore, a 1-ounce serving (just over 28 grams) of a food containing 20 grams of refined grains or other ingredients and 8 grams of whole-grain ingredients does not constitute a full whole-grain serving. Conversely, a serving of a particular food containing 16 or more grams of whole-grain ingredients and 12 grams or less of other ingredients is equal to one whole-grain serving.

The Dietary Guidelines recommend three to six servings of whole grains each day for women aged 14 to 50 years, and three to five-and-a-half servings for women aged 51 years and over. The requirements for men are slightly higher: males aged 14 to 18 years and those aged 31 to 50 years should aim for three-and-a-half to seven servings per day; males aged 19 to 30 years should increase this to 4 to 8 servings per day; and males aged 51 years and over should aim for three to six servings per day.

To make things a little easier, the Whole Grains Council has introduced a labeling system that verifies the whole-grain content of particular foods. Products that bear the "100% Whole Grain" label (or "stamp") contain a complete serving of whole grains. Those that bear the "Whole Grain" stamp contain at least half a serving of whole grains. This system takes much of the guesswork out of assessing foods for their protein content but is not yet being used on all whole-grain foods.

Always favor foods made with whole-grain ingredients over refined ingredients, and as a rough guide, regard a 1-ounce serving of a whole-grain food as being about equal to one 16-gram serving of whole grains (allowing for the fact that other non-grain ingredients are likely to comprise the remaining 12 grams).

Cereal Grains

The grains that have been dietary staples since ancient times are actually edible grass seeds. They are often referred to as the cereal grains to distinguish them from inedible varieties and non-cereal seeds such as sesame, poppy, and pumpkin, which are commonly just called "seeds."

The eight main cereal grains are wheat, corn, rice, oats, rye, barley, sorghum, and a large group of small grains collectively known as "millet." They have all long been valued as

easy to store and transport, taking up little space and being light in weight. This suited the needs of nomadic tribes. As dried seeds, they could be stored for lengthy periods to sustain more settled communities when fresh food was scarce. (Additional cereal grains include teff, wild rice, and triticale, which is a hybrid of wheat and rye.)

One of the main features of cereal grasses is that they are monocots, meaning they bear one-seeded fruits. The fruits of the grass are commonly called kernels, grains, or berries.

Barley (*Hordeum vulgare*)

Barley is one of the oldest cultivated grains—its domestication dates to 9000 BC in parts of Asia and Europe. Eventually it spread more widely on account of its ability to tolerate diverse climates and conditions. Like many grains, it was not introduced into North America until after the arrival of Columbus.

Historically, barley was used as a food for both animals and humans, but in more recent times, its most favored use has probably been as one of the key ingredients in beer. The malt in beer is derived from barley during a process that converts its starch into maltose.

Barley grains are widely available, either in the whole-grain form, known as hulled barley, which includes the outer hull, or pearled barley, which has had the hull removed.

Barley is popular as an alternative to wheat because it is nutritious and easily digested. It also has less gluten than wheat, but is not suitable for those with celiac disease.

Besides being an excellent source of energy-giving carbs, barley is also high in protein. It is a good source of molybdenum, manganese, dietary fiber, selenium, copper, vitamin B1, chromium, phosphorus, magnesium, and niacin. Barley's dietary fiber is high in beta-glucan, which is known to help lower cholesterol. Other compounds found in barley also help lower cholesterol and reduce inflammation.

Barley grows in a field.

As well as its use in beer, barley has long been a popular ingredient in soups and stews. Once cooked, it has a creamy, chewy texture. In soups and other hot foods, it traps flavors, and then releases them gently upon eating, all the while complementing the other flavors with a mild nutty taste. As it expands, barley also works as a thickener and adds a richness to the dish. It works particularly well with broths in this way. Soup made with chicken broth, barley, and other vegetables is an

Fast Fact

Barley is not often used in baking unless it is combined with other flours. This is because it is low in gluten, so it does not rise well, even if yeast is added.

Fast Fact

Refined barley, known as pearl barley, does not lose as much fiber or as many nutrients during the hulling process as other grains do. As a result, pearl barley is almost as nutritious as the whole-grain version, known as pot barley or Scotch barley, which is time-consuming to prepare and requires soaking.

enduring classic—simple, nutritious, and delicious.

Barley also works well in salads, in place of wheat in tabbouleh or rice in rice salads, where it pockets the dressing and traps its flavor. Ground barley appears in baked goods, but because it has less gluten than wheat, barley flour leads to heavier, more dense baked goods. The flour can be mixed with other flours and leaveners if lighter baked goods are desired.

Facing page: A barley field in Thailand.
Below: Classic chicken and barley soup.

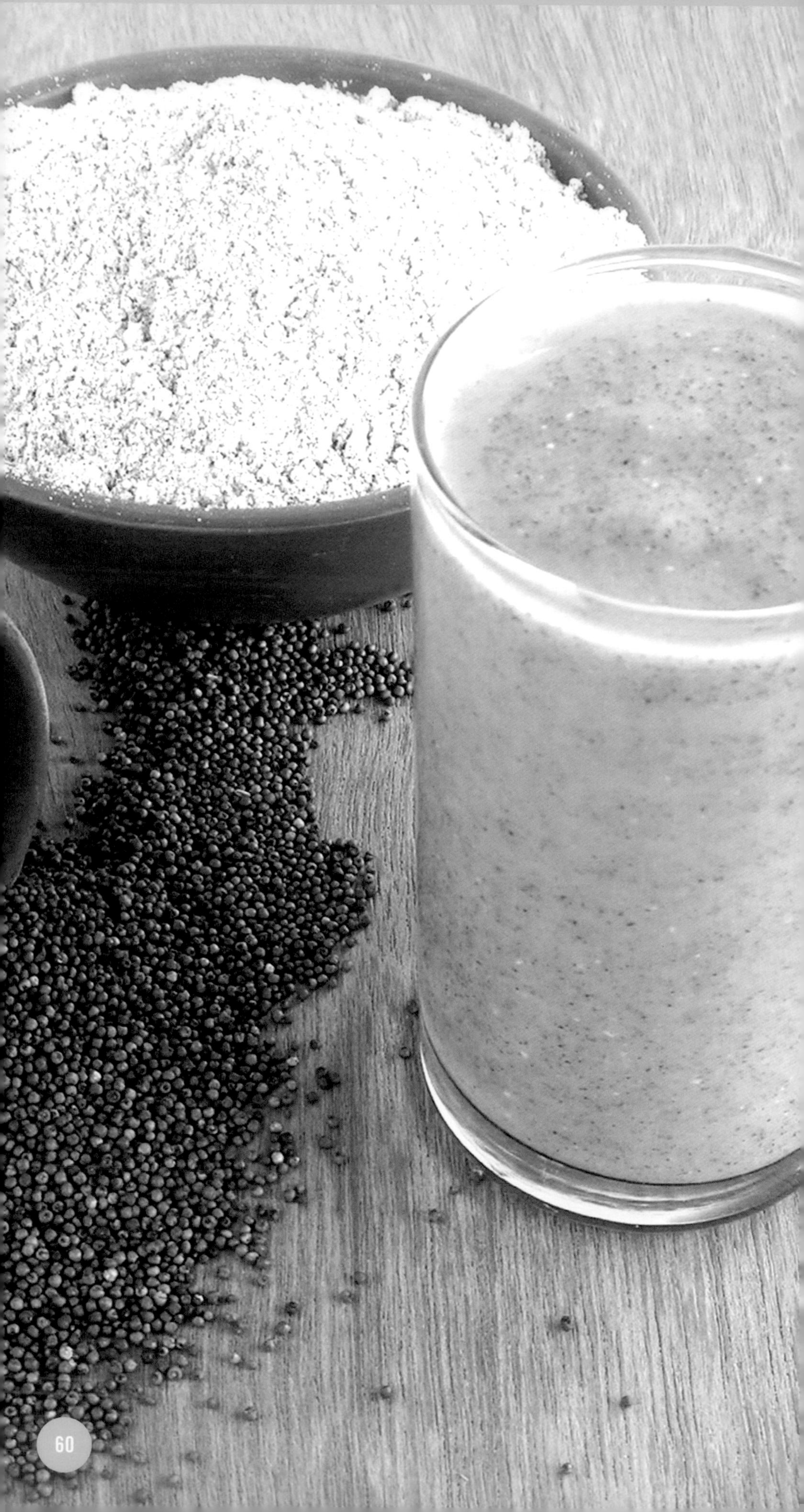

Finger Millet

(*Eleusine corocana*)

Fast Fact

Finger millet is an excellent source of calcium.

Known as *ragi* in India, finger millet is native to Africa and was introduced to India around 1000 BC. It is so named because the seed head usually has five spikes, or "fingers," that radiate from a central point. Today it is widely cultivated in many African countries, including Uganda, Ethiopia, and Zimbabwe; in the Indian states of Andhra Prades and Tamil Nad; and in parts of Asia. Finger millet grows best in cool, elevated regions and needs more water than other millets. The Indian variety of finger millet has long spikes, as opposed to the

Facing page: Finger millet hot cereal.
Right: Raw finger millet noodles.
Below: Indian finger millet.

shorter, more curved fingers of the African variety.

When used as a food, finger millet is usually ground into a flour and used to make Indian flatbreads such as *roti* and *batloo*, or leavened breads and *ragi dosa,* a delicious, thin Indian pancake.

In Africa, it is often eaten as a gritty hot cereal, used for brewing beer, or appears as an ingredient in soups and stews.

Top left: African finger millet.

Left: Indian finger millet.

Below: Ragi dosa pancake.

Facing page: Finger millet soup.

Foxtail Millet

(Setaria italica)

Foxtail millet is so named because of the foxtail-like appearance of its seed head. Like proso millet (page 82), it is valued as both a food for humans and as stock feed, and was originally cultivated in China 5,000 to 6,000 years ago. It is now a primary food crop in that country's drier northern regions. Foxtail millet is also grown in India, Indonesia, and parts of Korea and southern Europe. It is not grown in significant quantities in Africa.

Foxtail millet is usually cooked like rice and served as an accompaniment to curries or as an ingredient in spicy vegetable concoctions. As a flour, it appears in breads and other baked goods, and operates as a thickening agent in stews, soups, and sauces.

Fast Fact

Foxtail millet is the oldest cultivated millet, and millets are the oldest cultivated crop.

Facing page: Partially dried foxtail millet.

Below: Young foxtail millet.

What Is Millet?

Millet is the general term given to a group of small-seeded cereal grasses that are not closely related and do not belong to the wheat, barley, oats, maize, or rice families. There are many different varieties that are cultivated as food for both humans and animals around the world and that can be divided into two broad categories: pearl millet, which is the most widely grown of all millets, and small millets. As the name might suggest, most (but not all) of the small millet varieties have smaller grains than pearl millet.

All millets are gluten-free, which makes them a good choice for those who suffer from celiac disease and certain other dietary conditions. The different types provide various amounts of protein, with pearl millet offering the most. Like most other grains, however, the millets do not provide complete protein and lack the amino acid lysine. They are, nonetheless, a rich source of energy-giving carbohydrates.

Four of the most popular types of millets are discussed separately in this book: see page 61 for more information on finger millet, page 65 for foxtail millet, page 78 for pearl millet, and page 82 for proso millet.

Grains of yellow proso millet.

There are also several other varieties of millet that, although less significant globally, are important in their regions. These include barnyard millet of the tropical and subtropical regions of India, Japan, and other areas; little millet, widely cultivated in Nepal, Pakistan, India, and parts of Indonesia and Myanmar; kodo millet of western Africa and India; Job's tears of southeast Asia; and black fonio, white fonio, and Guinea millets of the dry regions of western Africa.

Although not generally considered to be a type of millet, sorghum is somewhat confusingly also referred to as "great millet." It is discussed on page 96.

From top: Barnyard millet and black fonio millet.

Left: Job's tears: stalks and hot cereal.

Maize/Corn (*Zea mays*)

This grain, commonly referred to as corn, has its origins in Central and South America and appears to have been first cultivated in parts of Mexico sometime around 5000 BC. In the late fifteenth century, Christopher Columbus introduced it to Europe, where it spread quickly southeast and into northern Africa before finding its way to China, the Far East, the Philippines, and Australia. Today, corn is the world's third most important grain for human consumption, after wheat and rice. It is also used extensively in other ways, including fuel production, plastics manufacturing, pharmaceuticals, and stock feed.

Corn has very large seed heads, known as cobs or ears, that can grow up to two feet in height. Hundreds of seeds, known as kernels, encircle each cob. They

are most commonly yellow or white, but may also be orange, red, blue, purple, brown, or black.

In today's varieties of corn, each cob and its kernel is contained within a large husk formed by long leaves that both protects the kernels and prevents them from being naturally distributed. Hence, human intervention and cultivation are required to grow further crops.

Of the many varieties of corn, four are the most widely recognized and cultivated. These are discussed below.

Dent Corn

Dent corn, also known as field corn, is so named because of the dimple that forms in the kernel as it dries out. It is higher in starch and less sweet than sweet corn. Field corn is typically used as animal feed, in manufacturing, and

Fast Fact

Popcorn, which explodes when heated, is available in white, yellow, red, and black kernels. They need to be cured before they can be popped. One suggested method is to place cobs in a mesh bag and store them in a warm, dry, well-ventilated place such as a garage for three or four weeks while the outer shell hardens. You can tell if the kernels are ready to pop by twisting the cob firmly: if the kernels drop off easily, it's time to heat the pan.

Dent corn.

Fast Fact

Unlike most other cereal grains, where only one kernel is found inside the tough outer husk, a hundred or more corn kernels are found within the hull formed by the tough outer leaves. But each of those kernels, technically individual fruits, contains only one seed.

for making corn syrup, breakfast cereals, popcorn, and corn flour.

Flint Corn

Flint corn, also known as Indian corn, is the small-grained, hard-shelled, and multicolored "hard-as-flint" type. It has a decorative appearance, but is used as animal feed and can be ground into flour, becoming the basis for various dishes and snacks, including polenta (grits), tortillas, corn chips, and popcorn.

Flour Corn

This type of corn has large, soft, starchy grains that can be ground easily and are used to produce cornmeal, a thickening agent that can be added to sauces, curries, and gravies.

Sweet Corn

The most popular of the corn varieties is the sweet and juicy yellow or white sweet corn that is enjoyed as corn on the cob all around the world—boiled, steamed, grilled, or baked. The kernels are also removed from the cob and used in salads and other dishes.

In terms of nutrition, all corn is a good source of carbs

and of various vitamins and minerals, but its most important role may be as a gluten-free alternative to other grains. Hence it is of high importance in the celiac diet. It also provides good amounts of fiber. Corn lacks at least two essential amino acids, however, and so is an incomplete source of protein. It should be combined with other complementary proteins to ensure a proper nutritional balance.

Corn syrup and high-fructose corn syrup are both produced from cornstarch. Pure corn syrup is almost 100 percent glucose and has very little fructose. It is an alternative to table sugar (sucrose) and, like table sugar, should be avoided or used only in moderation. High-fructose corn syrup is the subject of much controversy. It has much higher levels of fructose and glucose, and is thought by some to be a contributing factor to the Western world's obesity epidemic. Other studies suggest that it might lead to feelings of hunger and prevent satiety. Research to date, however, is inconclusive, with insufficient evidence to confirm that high-fructose corn syrup poses greater problems than table sugar. The best rule of thumb is to limit the consumption of all types of sugar.

All types of corn are used in many dishes and products—even

Mexican tacos with corn tortillas, chicken, and beans.

Fast Fact

Colorful Indian corn.

to make bourbon whiskey. Popular whole-grain dishes include corn on the cob and popcorn. The whole kernels are also used in salads, stews, and soups, or simply mixed with other vegetables and grains.

Corn (either wet- or dry-milled) can also be ground to various degrees of fineness. The more coarse, dry grinds are used to make grits, polenta, and cornbread, whereas the finely ground flours are preferred for baked goods. Hominy is food produced from dried corn kernels that have undergone a process called nixtamilization (to release the corn's niacin) and is in turn also used to create masa, a corn-based dough used to make tortillas, tacos, and similar products.

Corn and Pellagra

During the first half of the 20th century, scientists established a link between diets high in corn and incidents of pellagra, a disease caused by a niacin deficiency. Although corn contained niacin (vitamin B3), it was in what is known as bound form and is not absorbed by the human body. Hence, pellagra was common in the United States in the 1940s, particularly among people for whom corn was a dietary staple.

It did not, however, afflict the corn-eating Native Americans. At first, this mystery could not be explained, but eventually scientists found that the Native Americans employed the process of nixtamilization, which includes treating corn with an alkali substance such as limewater or ash. This releases the niacin into the food.

John Smith Negotiating for Corn
By Sidney King

Fast Fact

Of the cereal grains, oats contain the highest amount of protein.

Oats (*Avena sativa*)

Oats are perhaps best known as the main ingredient of oatmeal. Oats have long been Scotland's principal cereal crop, and they feature in much of that country's fare—including haggis, the national dish, which traditionally comprises a sheep's stomach stuffed with minced organ meat and oatmeal.

Oats have been cultivated for both human and animal consumption in Europe and Asia since ancient times. They were not grown in North America until the early 1600s, but once they arrived, they flourished. In the late nineteenth century, German American Ferdinand Schumacher developed precooked, flaked oats that proved very popular and were later packaged by Henry Crowell under the Quaker Oats brand.

Oats have the highest protein content of all true cereals, and are also rich in other nutrients, especially vitamin E, some B vitamins, and minerals such as zinc, manganese, and silica. They also contain certain antioxidants

Top left: Dried oats.
Bottom left: Oat grass growing in the field.
Facing page: Oats with nuts and fruit.

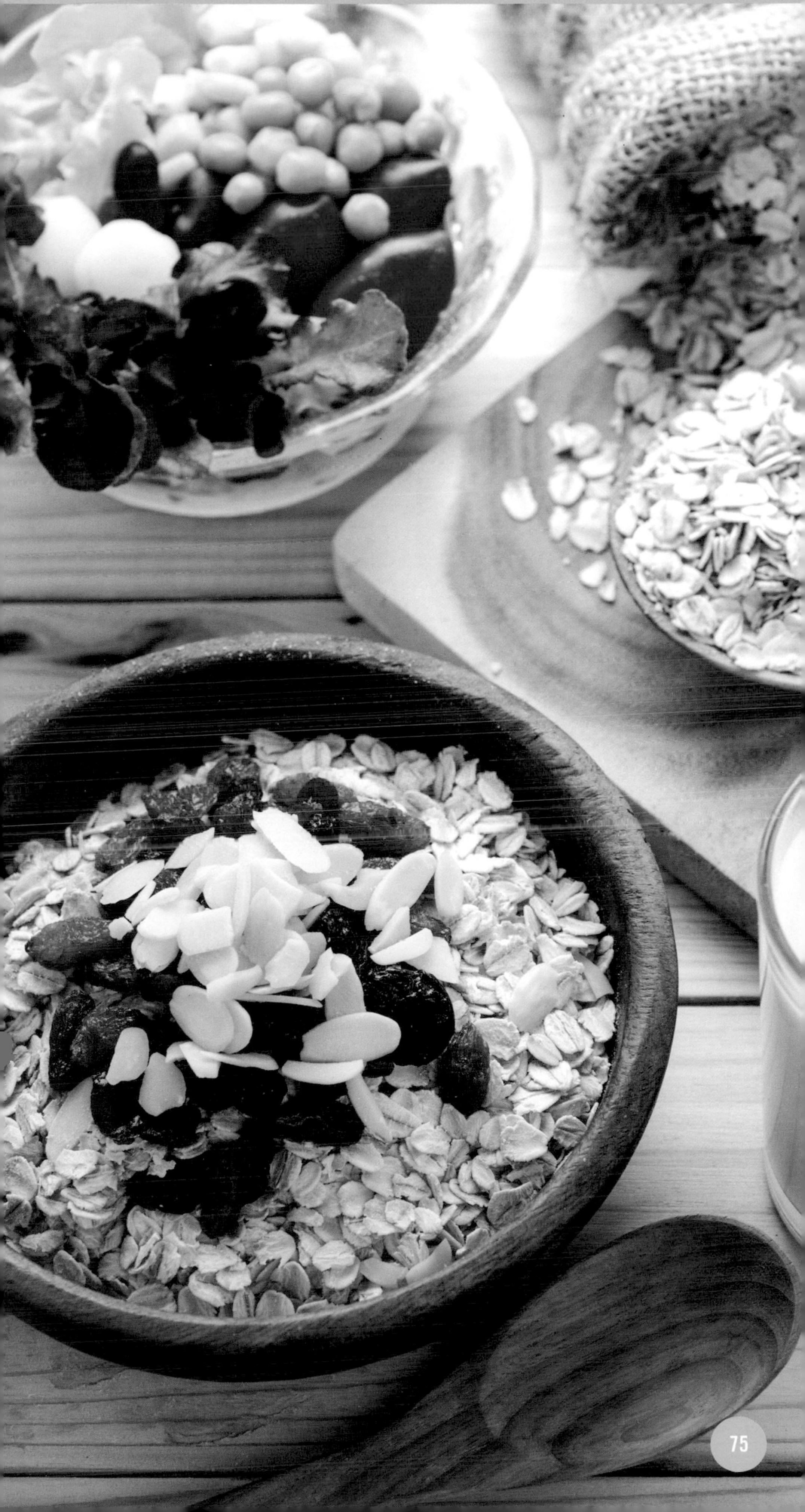

Top: Oat cookies with sesame, sunflower, and amaranth.

Above: Fresh bread made from oats and grains.

Fast Fact

Oats have a high moisture content (about 14 percent). The moisture is removed by drying and usually lightly toasting the oats while they are processed.

that may help reduce the risk of inflammatory diseases. Oats are high in fiber, particularly a fiber known as beta-glucan. This has been shown to reduce cholesterol levels, which in turn reduces the risk of cardiovascular disease and stroke. Oats are also currently being researched for their antioxidant properties, which may have additional positive impacts on cholesterol. Like most cereal grains, oats are not a complete protein.

The oats available in stores include steel-cut oats, rolled oats, quick-cooking oats, and instant oats. Steel-cut oats are often considered more nutritious because they are the least processed, but they need to be cooked for up to 45 minutes before they can be eaten.

Rolled oats and quick-cooking oats are steamed and rolled, and so are quicker to cook. Instant oats are heavily processed and dehydrated, and considerably less nutritious than other types.

The term "oatmeal" generally refers to raw oats that have been cut or ground in various grades from coarse (for example, steel-cut oats) to fine, and need to be cooked prior to eating.

Oat flour is made of finely ground oats, which are naturally gluten-free but do contain a glutenlike protein known as avenin. Although avenin may be more easily tolerated by those with gluten sensitivities than gluten, oats are not generally recommended for people with celiac disease for this reason. Even oats labeled as gluten-free are most likely to contain avenin. Oats also run a high risk of cross-contamination with products that do contain gluten.

As a breakfast food, oats are also eaten raw or toasted in mueslis and cereals, combined whole or as flour into bread, and used in a wide range of other baked goods. Oats have a wholesome, slightly earthy flavor that complements sweet flavors such as honey and maple syrup. They also work well with savory spices and flavors, such as cinnamon.

Fast Fact

Face masks made from oatmeal are used as home beauty treatments. Supposedly the oats remove dead skin cells and soak up excess oil, thereby helping to treat acne.

Oats with berries

Fast Fact

Millet, barley, soybeans, rice, and wheat are considered the five sacred crops of China.

Pearl Millet

(*Pennisetum glaucum*)

Pearl millet, also known as bullrush millet, bajar, gero, and sanio, among other names, is native to the drier tropical regions of Africa and Asia. It was probably first cultivated approximately 3,000 years ago. It grows well in poor-quality, sandy soil, even in drought and intense heat, and is one of the most drought-resistant of all grains. While it varies in color from red tones to gray and black, it is most commonly gray, hence the name pearl millet.

Pearl millet is a common ingredient in bird food, but it is also a delicious cereal that can be ground and cooked like oatmeal, or used as the flour for a range of leavened breads and flatbreads popular in Africa and India. It is sometimes used in place of cracked wheat and other grains in salads and side dishes.

Pearl millet comes in several delicious flavors. Once cooked, its texture varies from something resembling creamy mashed potatoes to fluffy rice.

Facing page: Pearl millet.
Left: Pearl millet left to dry on the plant.

In terms of health, some research indicates that pearl millet may be of special benefit to women. Recent studies have indicated a link between the consumption of pearl millet and a reduced incidence of gallstones in women. It is also thought that pearl millet, if eaten regularly, may provide some protection against certain types of breast cancer. Although more research is needed in these areas, the results to date seem promising.

Millets and Goiter

One potential health risk associated with millet concerns compounds called goitrogens. When consumed in large quantities, these so-called anti-nutrients interfere with the thyroid's absorption of iodine and can cause a disorder called goiter, an enlarged thyroid gland. Although some consumption of millet and other foods containing goitrogens (soybeans and flaxseed are two more) should not cause this problem, high consumption of goitrogen-containing foods may trigger or worsen an existing thyroid problem. For this reason, millet should just be part of a variety of grains included in a healthy diet, rather than a staple. Anyone concerned about his or her thyroid health should consult with a medical practitioner about foods to limit or eliminate entirely from the diet.

A Case of Goitre
By Thomas Boyle Grierson

Facing page: Millet soup.

Fast Fact

Proso millet is the only millet crop grown in the United States.

Proso Millet
(*Panicum miliaceum*)

Proso millet, also known as common millet, Indian millet, and hog millet, is widely cultivated across the globe. The seeds are generally cream or red. It has an untidy appearance, with drooping seed heads called panicles. These panicles are also used in cleaning supplies—one of the traditional uses is to make the brush on a broom. For this reason, proso millet is sometimes called broom millet.

Proso millet is native to China, but has been widely cultivated for over 5,000 years throughout Asia and the Middle East, as well as in many parts of Europe. It subsequently spread to the Americas and Australia. As a crop, it has a low water requirement and adapts well to various soil and climatic conditions, including the mountainous regions of Russia and China. It is generally

Broom with broomhead made from millet stalks.

82

considered to be easy to grow. Proso millet is most commonly eaten as a hot cereal. Ground into a flour, it is also used as a gluten-free alternative in the preparation of flatbreads and salads such as tabbouleh, and for brewing beer. It is a highly regarded stockfeed for cattle and pigs, and a common ingredient in birdseed.

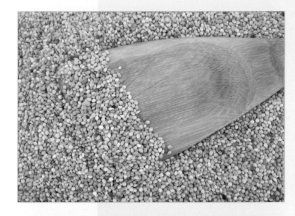

Top: Proso millet.
Above: Red common millet with husks.
Below: Hot cereal made
from foxtail millet.

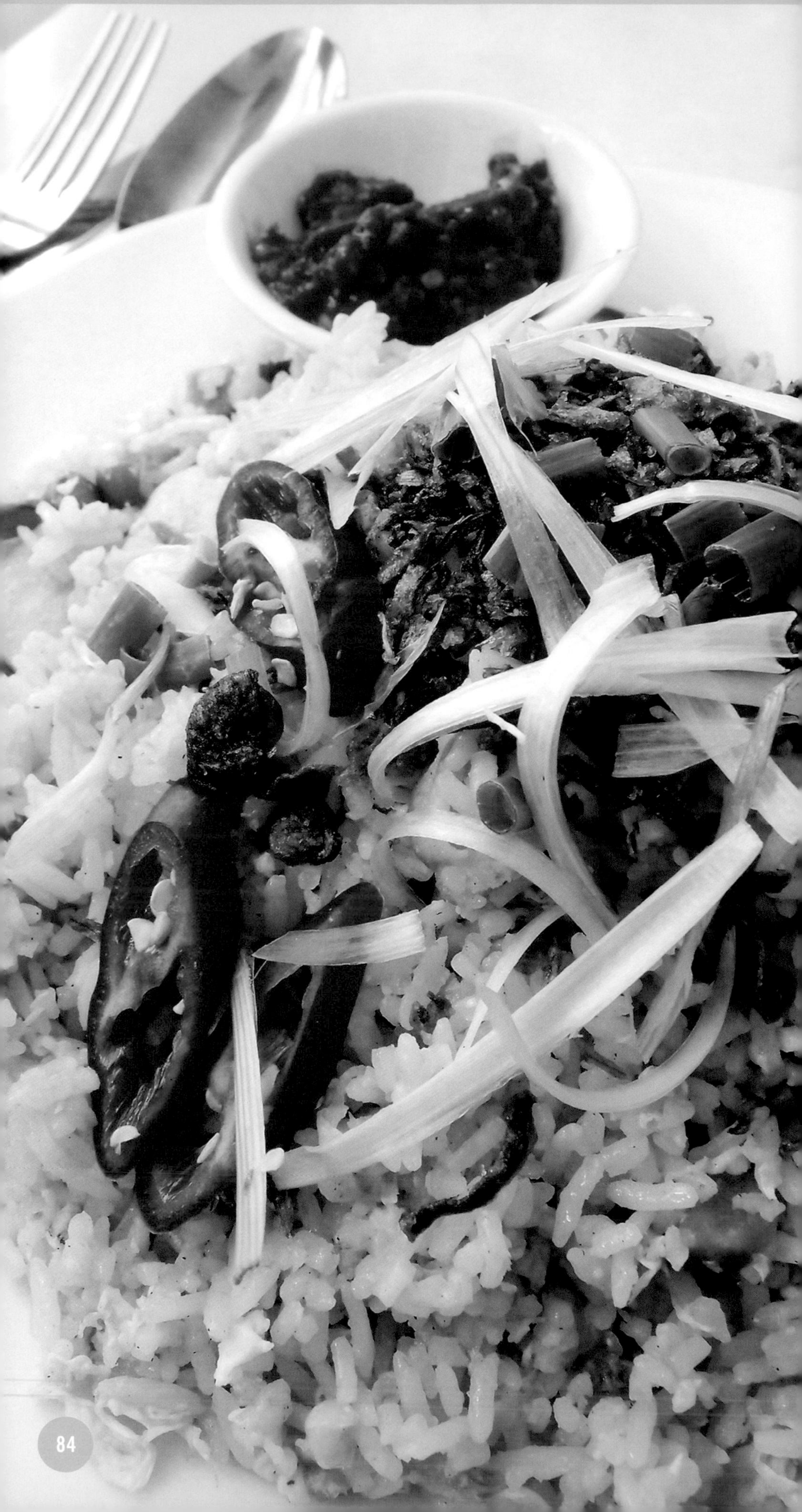

Rice (*Oryza sativa*)

This versatile grain is a food staple around the world. It is also widely used as an accompaniment to or ingredient in many dishes, both savory and sweet.

Like many other grains, rice has been cultivated since Neolithic times—first in parts of Asia before spreading to Europe, Africa, and then eventually North America in the seventeenth century.

Of the tens of thousands of varieties of rice in the world, each falls into either the long- or short-grain category. The long-grain varieties (such as basmati have long, slender grains that stay separate after cooking This is due to the presence of high amounts of a starch called amylose that does not gelatinize or become sticky when cooked. On the other hand, the rounder, short-grain varieties (such as, sushi or Japanese rice) have lower levels of amylose but higher levels of another starch, amylopectin, that becomes sticky upon cooking. Some short-grain varieties such as sticky, glutinous, or sweet rice have no amylose at all and

Facing page: Asian-style fried rice.

Fast Fact

Rice is thrown at weddings because it is a symbol of life and fertility.

Fast Fact

Rice is the main food source for more than half of the world's population.

Below: From top, uncooked, basmati, arborio, and jasmine rice.

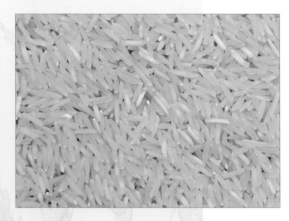

the highest amounts of amylopectin, so they are used in the rice desserts favored in some Asian cuisines.

The short-grain rices of the Mediterranean, such as arborio and canaroli, sometimes referred to as medium-grain rice, contain moderate amounts of amylose and amylopectin. Together these provide the creamy yet firm qualities of risotto and similar dishes.

Brown rice is raw rice that has not been milled, so it retains its bran and germ. White rice is brown rice that has been milled to remove its outer husk and germ, and is sometimes further polished. Nutritionally, rice is high in carbohydrates, making it an important source of energy for much of the world's population. Long-grain rice, or rice that has more amylose than amylopectin, has a lower glycemic index than white short-grain rice, and so is generally considered to be a healthier option, especially for people with diabetes or other blood-sugar disorders. Rice also contains good amounts of protein and various vitamins and minerals, and no fat other than small amounts found in the germ and in the bran.

Brown rice is more nutritious than white because many vitamins and minerals are found in the husk. Both the germ and the husk also provide much-needed fiber. It does, however, take a lot longer to cook than white rice and, due to the presence of oils in the husk, has a shorter shelf life.

Rice bran is a rich source of fiber, and is readily available in health food stores and some supermarkets. Rice bran oil is extracted from rice bran and is high in antioxidants, healthy fats, and other nutrients. It is light in flavor and does not smoke too much at high temperatures, making it ideal for cooking. It also emulsifies easily, making it a nice addition to salad dressings.

Fast Fact

Distilled rice plants are used to make *sake*, a Japanese liquor.

Below: From top, uncooked brown whole-grain rice, waxy or glutinous brown rice, and black glutinous rice.

Fast Facts

Rice was added to the walls of medieval Chinese structures to add strength and stability.

Rice is also gluten-free, and makes a wonderful substitute for wheat, barley, and other grains for those who cannot tolerate gluten. It is a low-allergen food, hence its suitability as a first food for infants.

Plain, boiled rice is a staple in many parts of the world, but it is also served alongside countless other dishes, particularly those with sauces and gravies, because of its ability to mop up the tasty liquids. Such dishes include curries, casseroles, and stews. It is also popular in fried rice dishes, paellas,

Terraced rice fields in Thailand.

risottos, and salads, which all consist of rice being mixed together with other ingredients, including combinations of vegetables, eggs, meat, chicken, fish, and flavored sauces.

Plain white long-grain rice has a clean, light flavor that makes it the perfect accompaniment to rich or spicy flavors, and also for the more delicate and subtle flavors of herbs and certain spices. The short-grain varieties tend to have a slightly sweet and sometimes fruity flavor. Additionally, rice is a key

Fast Fact

More than 40,000 varieties of rice are grown around the globe.

Rice Must Be Stored Correctly and Washed!

One problem with rice is that it can carry a bacterium called *Bacillus cereus*, which can survive cooking and lead to food poisoning. This can be prevented if cooked rice that is not eaten right away is refrigerated promptly. When rice is left to sit at room temperature, the bacteria will multiply rapidly and become toxic. Rice should also be washed thoroughly before cooking. In the case of certain prepared rice dishes such as sushi, however, the combination of sugar and vinegar has microbial properties that kill the bacteria, usually making such foods safe to eat.

Above: Coconut and mango rice pudding.

Fast Fact

In Japan, short-grain rice is the main ingredient of sushi.

ingredient in the Japanese seaweed rolls known as sushi, as well as in desserts. The sticky, short-grain varieties are favored for this purpose. Brown rice has a slightly nutty flavor.

Rice is also used to make breakfast cereals, crackers, biscuits, rice papers in which to wrap other ingredients, and even beer and wine, made from fermented rice. In addition, it can be ground into a gluten-free flour for baked goods, or used as a thickener.

Facing page: Rice paper rolls filled with vegetables.
Below: Spinach risotto.

Rye (*Secale cereale*)

Wild rye originated in parts of western Asia and northern Europe. It was first cultivated during the Neolithic period, but this may have been accidental. Some historians think that it appeared first as a weed among cultivated wheat and barley crops, but inadvertently produced a higher yield than the other two grains, so it became its own useful crop.

Later, rye's cultivation became significant during Roman times, when its ability to grow in the colder months and in lower-quality fields was well matched with the higher food demands imposed by the growing population.

During the Middle Ages, rye was the most popular bread grain consumed in Europe, and it remains a favorite in many parts of northern and eastern Europe and in North America, where it became an important bread crop in the late 1700s. The countries of Europe still grow

Facing page: Sliced dark rye bread.
Right: Rye growing in the field.

Below: Ear of rye with grains.

Fast Fact

Rye is generally available in whole-grain form that retains its nutrients, rather than refined, because it is difficult to separate the endosperm from the bran and germ.

and consume the most rye. It is sometimes called the "grain of poverty" because it can grow in poor conditions.

Rye is a hardy, tasty grain that is thought by some to be nutritionally superior to wheat. It is high in carbohydrates and protein, as well as various vitamins and minerals. It is relatively low in gluten compared to wheat, which may make it more suitable for people with certain food sensitivities or intolerances, but it is not suitable for those with celiac disease.

Rye is most commonly used as an ingredient in bread, of which there are four main types: light rye, dark rye, pumpernickel, and marbled. Generally, the darker the bread, the more nutritious it is, because it is more likely to include the grain's nutritious husk and germ. These are removed, for example, from the light rye variety.

True dark rye is dark on account of its whole-grain make up, but sometimes the darker color can be the result

Top left: Rye flour.
Center: Rye flour and grains.
Left: Sliced pumpernickel.

of coloring agents, such as molasses, added to a light rye flour. Pumpernickel is a dark, coarse bread that uses a more coarsely ground whole-grain flour. Marbled rye is a blend of different colored doughs that have been rolled or plaited together.

Rye has a strong, slightly sour taste that lends itself well to savory toppings such as cured meats, smoked seafood, pickles, and cheese. Its low amount of gluten results in a denser, heavier food, to which its flavor and texture are well suited.

Rye bagel.

Fast Fact

The first bagels date from 1610 in Poland. They were a gift for women after childbirth.

Polish sour rye soup.

Fast Fact

Benjamin Franklin likely introduced sorghum into the United States.

Below: Sorghum and carrot soup; stalks of sorghum.

Sorghum (*Sorghum bicolor*)

This is a cereal grain native to the tropical regions of all continents around the globe. It is also known by various other names, including great millet, milo, and guinea corn. Sorghum was first cultivated in southern Egypt some 8,000 years ago, before spreading through Africa and then later into India around 1000 BC. It probably reached North America sometime in the seventeenth century.

As the world's fifth most important crop, sorghum is a staple food in the dry climates of northern Africa, India, and parts of Central America, where it grows well under hot, arid conditions. Elsewhere, it

is used primarily as animal feed, for producing ethanol, and in manufacturing. One particular variety, broom corn, is cultivated to make brooms, in the same way millet brooms have been made for centuries. Other varieties are used in China and elsewhere for brewing beer, and in the United States as a substitute for maple syrup.

In recent times, sorghum has been more accepted as a quality food source in North America, likely on account of its nutritious properties. As well as being gluten-free, it is high in certain antioxidants that may help reduce the incidence of cancers and cardiovascular diseases.

An area of particular interest concerns sorghum's waxy compounds known as policosanols. Although research is not yet conclusive, these compounds may help reduce cholesterol, among other benefits, and so may help in the prevention, treatment, and management of some cardiovascular conditions.

Fast Fact

Sweet sorghum is the concentrated, pure juice of sorghum cane. In some parts of the United States, it is called "sorghum molasses" or sometimes simply "molasses." But true molasses refers to a syrup produced from sugarcane or sugar beets.

Below: Sorghum grains; sorghum after harvesting.

Sorghum is also used in various food preparations as a gluten-free flour. Its flavor is similar to buckwheat and can be cooked as a hot cereal, mixed into salads like couscous, or even used to make flatbreads such as the *chapati* and *roti* of Asia.

Top: Sorghum growing in a field.
Left: Sorghum molasses on a muffin.

What Are the Main Parts of a Grain?

In terms of food, the main parts of a grain are the outer, protective hull (or husk), the bran, the endosperm, and the germ. (Other parts include the pericarp, seed coat, and aleuron.)

Hull/Husk: The outer, inedible casing of the grain.

Glume: The coarse, leaflike structures (also known as **bracts**) that form the hull. Usually, two glumes form the hull.

Bran: The outer protective layer of the grain. A concentrated source of fiber, it also contains several nutrients, but in most cases, the body cannot use them unless they've been heated or cooked. Yeast leavening also helps.

Endosperm: The starchy tissue that surrounds the embryo or germ, and provides it with nourishment. We grind it into flour.

Germ: The tiny, nutritious plant embryo, a new plant in the making inside the grain.

Whole grains vs refined grains: Whole grains have had only their outer hulls removed and retain the bran and germ. Refined grains have had the hull, bran, and germ removed. Only the endosperm remains, causing many nutrients and fiber to be lost or depleted. (An exception is pearl barley, see page 56.)

Groats and Berries: Other terms for "whole grain."

Endosperm

Bran

Germ

Hulled grain: Whole grains that are fully enclosed by their tough, outer hulls. These must be removed by milling, and include barley, rye, and emmer. Others, such as bread wheat, are not, and can be threshed without milling to release the grain (see page 115).

Fast Fact

Unlike most other cereal grains, teff is a complete protein that contains all the essential amino acids. (Spelt is another complete protein.) Teff is also gluten-free.

Teff (*Eragrostis tef*)

The world's smallest cereal grain, teff is about the size of a poppy seed. It is indigenous to northern Africa, and is a staple of the Ethiopian diet. Teff is hardy, nutritious, and thrives in a range of climates and in diverse altitudes, from sea level to almost 10,000 feet. Hence it is now grown widely around the world, including in Europe, North America, Asia, and Australia.

Teff is a good source of carbohydrates and a complete source of protein—it contains all the essential amino acids that cannot be produced by the human body and must be sourced through food. It is gluten-free, and an excellent source of dietary fiber, calcium, and other nutrients. The dietary fiber found in teff is resistant starch, which provides a number of health benefits (see page 33).

Below: Teff growing in the field; teff grains.

Facing page: Ethiopian foods served with injera made from teff.

Injera

The most curious aspect of this flatbread is that it is used as a plate, or even a table, on which to spread an array of foods—but the "plate" or "table" is eaten as part of the feast. Usually made with teff or a mix of teff, sorghum, millet, and sometimes other grains, injera is a sourdough flatbread with yeast added. It has a fluffy, slightly spongy consistency and a sour, slightly tangy flavor. Injera can be topped with all kinds of foods, including salads, grains, pureed beans, eggs, and meats. It is also used to mop up stews and sauces, and is part of the national cuisine of Ethiopia and Eritrea.

Injera served with various dips.

Teff has a subtle, nutty flavor that works well when combined with or served alongside fragrant spices and other strong flavors. Generally, the darker grains are more strongly flavored than lighter varieties. Depending on how it is cooked, teff's texture can range from a creamy mix similar to mashed potatoes to individual grains that are about the same size as poppy seeds and are ideal for sprinkling on top of other dishes. Because teff is too small to process, it is always consumed as a whole grain, so it retains all the nutrients found in the germ and the bran. Teff is also ground into a flour that can be use for baked goods like pancakes and waffles. It is often the main ingredient in the Ethiopian flatbread *injera*, which has a slightly sour taste because it is traditionally made from a fermented (sour) dough of teff, sorghum, or a combination of both.

Fast Fact

Teff is thought to provide Ethiopians with about two-thirds of their dietary protein. Some long-distance runners from Ethiopia have attributed their success partly to the energy-giving and health-supporting features of this compact, nutritious grain.

Ethiopian flatbread made from teff.

Triticale (*Triticosecale* hybrids)

Triticale is a cultivated grain created by cross-fertilizing wheat and rye. Although it was first developed in the 1870s, the early seedlings were sterile, so it was not until the mid-20th century that advances in genetics enabled a fertile version to be produced. The hope was that triticale would produce a high-quality, nutritious alternative grain with the hardiness of rye and the bread-making qualities of wheat that would help solve many problems associated with poor-yielding crops, famine, and malnutrition around the world.

On its first commercial release in 1970, triticale was hailed as a "miracle," but the crops were disappointingly inconsistent, and acceptance in the marketplace was low. Interest soon faded.

The promise remains, however, as it continues to undergo further research and as development in the hope of improving its acceptance as a food for human consumption, and a type of fuel. Today, though, triticale is used primarily as an animal feed.

Fast Fact

Triticale has more dietary fiber, protein, and minerals than wheat or rye, but has been used primarily as stock feed and is not as widely produced as other grains. This is probably because its cultivation is initially more complex. However, the grain's impressive nutritional benefits are generating new interest in it as a food for humans.

Nutritionally, triticale is similar to wheat, and is a good source of carbs, vitamins, and minerals, including manganese, thiamin, and folate. It is also a reasonable source of protein, but like many grains lacks the essential amino acid lysine, so it is not a complete protein.

Although triticale has not been widely accepted as a food source, it is sometimes used to make various flours and breakfast cereals. Rolled whole-grain triticale makes a suitable substitute for rolled oats, while its flour can be used in breads, where it tends to take on a flavor and texture similar to light rye.

Left, from top: Triticale growing in the field; triticale grains; a feed truck unloads triticale grown for animal feed.

Facing page: A poppy grows in a field of triticale.

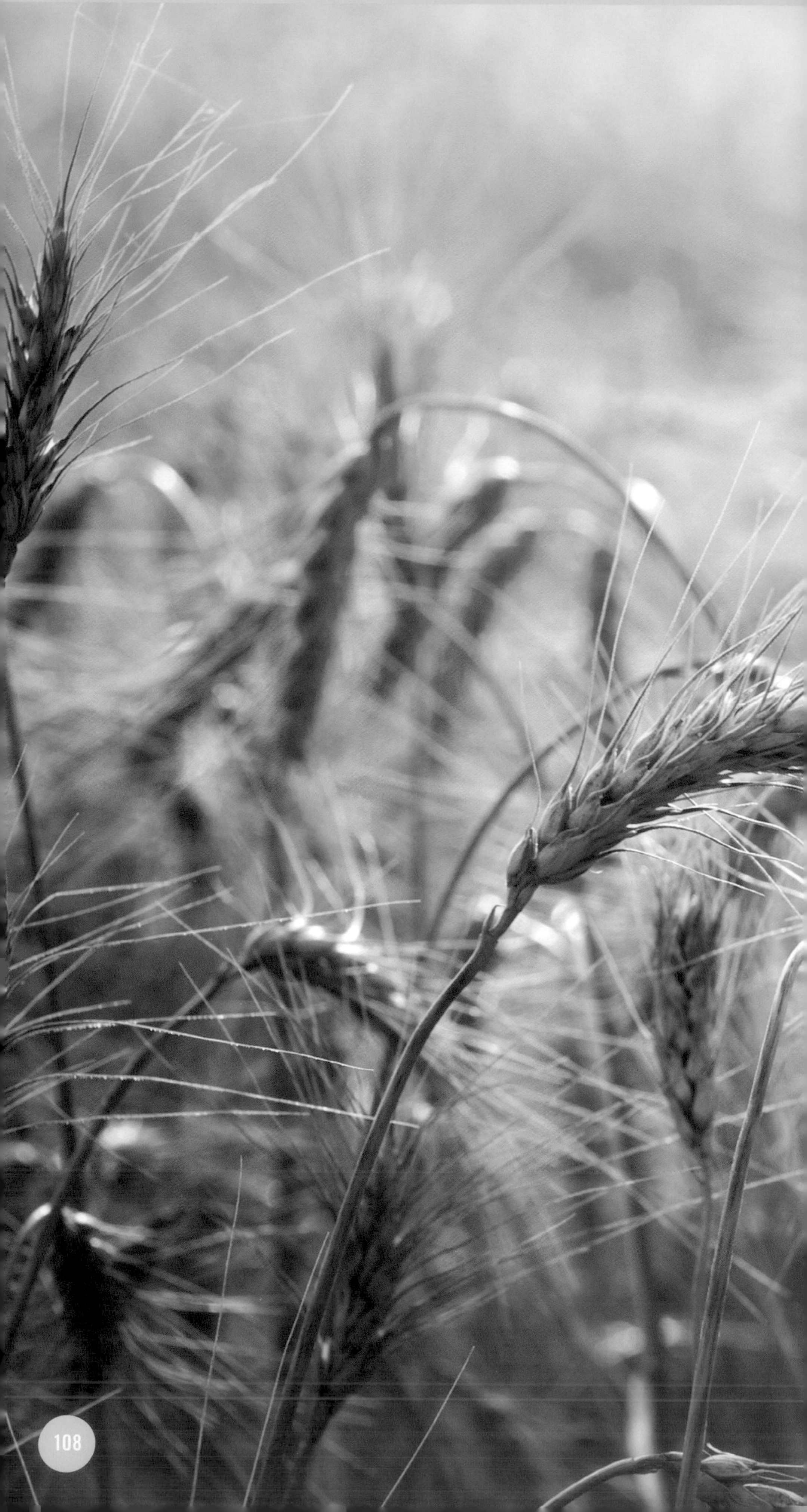

Wheat (*Triticum* ssp.)

Bread may be the staff of life—but before there was bread, there was wheat. It has been cultivated since at least 9000 BC, and remains a staple in many parts of the world. Originally cultivated in the Middle East, wheat spread across Europe, parts of Africa, and Asia as humans migrated during the Neolithic period and became the most important cereal crop for those early civilizations. It did not reach North America until the early 1600s.

The thousands of wheat varieties fall into four distinct groups according to their genetic makeup: einkorn wheat, one of the earliest types to be cultivated; durum wheat and the ancient grains emmer and Khorasan; bread wheat that, as the name suggests, is commonly used to make bread and baked goods; and the ancient grain spelt.

However, wheats are commonly divided simply into two broad groups: the modern and the ancient varieties. The former generally refers to two particular types, bread (or common) wheat, which accounts for about 95 percent of modern

Fast Fact

Refined flour, which has had both the germ and the bran removed, loses many of its nutrients, including the fiber and amino acid lysine in the bran; the vitamin E and B vitamins found in the germ, and various other minerals, including iron and zinc. White refined flour, produced from the starchy endosperm of the grain, is sometimes bleached during the manufacturing process, further depleting nutrients.

wheat production, and durum wheat for the other 5 percent. These are discussed on pages 115–18.

The term "ancient" refers to wheats that were cultivated in the early days of agriculture during the Neolithic period and that are now enjoying a resurgence in popularity due to their low levels of processing, nutritional qualities, and marketability. Ancient wheats include einkorn, emmer, spelt, and Khorasan wheat (sold as Kamut™). They are discussed separately in the "Ancient Grains" section (page 124). Other wheat-related foods include cracked or bulgur wheat, couscous, semolina, and farro, but these are actually types of prepared wheat, rather than distinct varieties.

Today, wheat is one of the most highly produced grains in the world. (Confusingly, buckwheat is not a wheat at

From top: Growing, harvesting, and separating wheat grains.

all. It is a plant related to sorrel and rhubarb.) All forms of wheat contain gluten, and the high levels of gluten found in wheat are part of the reasons for its widespread popularity. Gluten is a protein that gives wheat dough (wheat flour combined with water) elastic qualities and makes breads, cakes, and other baked goods chewy. Gluten also plays an important part in helping baked goods to rise: yeast creates gases that push the dough up and out. The more gluten in the dough, the more easily it stretches Gluten is a valuable food in itself, so much so that during the sixth century the Chinese developed a way to separate gluten from wheat to produce what is now known as *mien chin*, the "muscle of the flour" in Chinese, and *seitan* by the Japanese. On the other hand, as much as 8 percent of the world's population suffers

From top: Wheat flour, dough, buns, and a roll with burger.

Fast Fact

Wheatgrass, made from sprouted wheat, is often added to smoothies and juices. It is a good source of vitamins (including A, B-complex, C, and K) and minerals (including iron and zinc), incomplete protein, and chlorophyll (the green pigment found in plants). There are many claims regarding the health benefits of chloroyphll (among them blood strengthening and detoxification), but these have not yet been scientifically validated. Wheatgrass can also cause severe allergic reactions in some people.

from celiac disease, and another 8 percent may have some form of gluten intolerance.

Whole-grain wheat is an excellent source of energy-giving carbohydrates, incomplete protein, vitamins B and E, and fiber. Refined wheat, however, has a lower nutritional value and a higher glycemic index (see page 47). Wheat flour is used in countless breads and baked goods, and is also made into breakfast cereals. Wheat is also used in beer and for animal feed, and wheat products include refined starch and wheat germ.

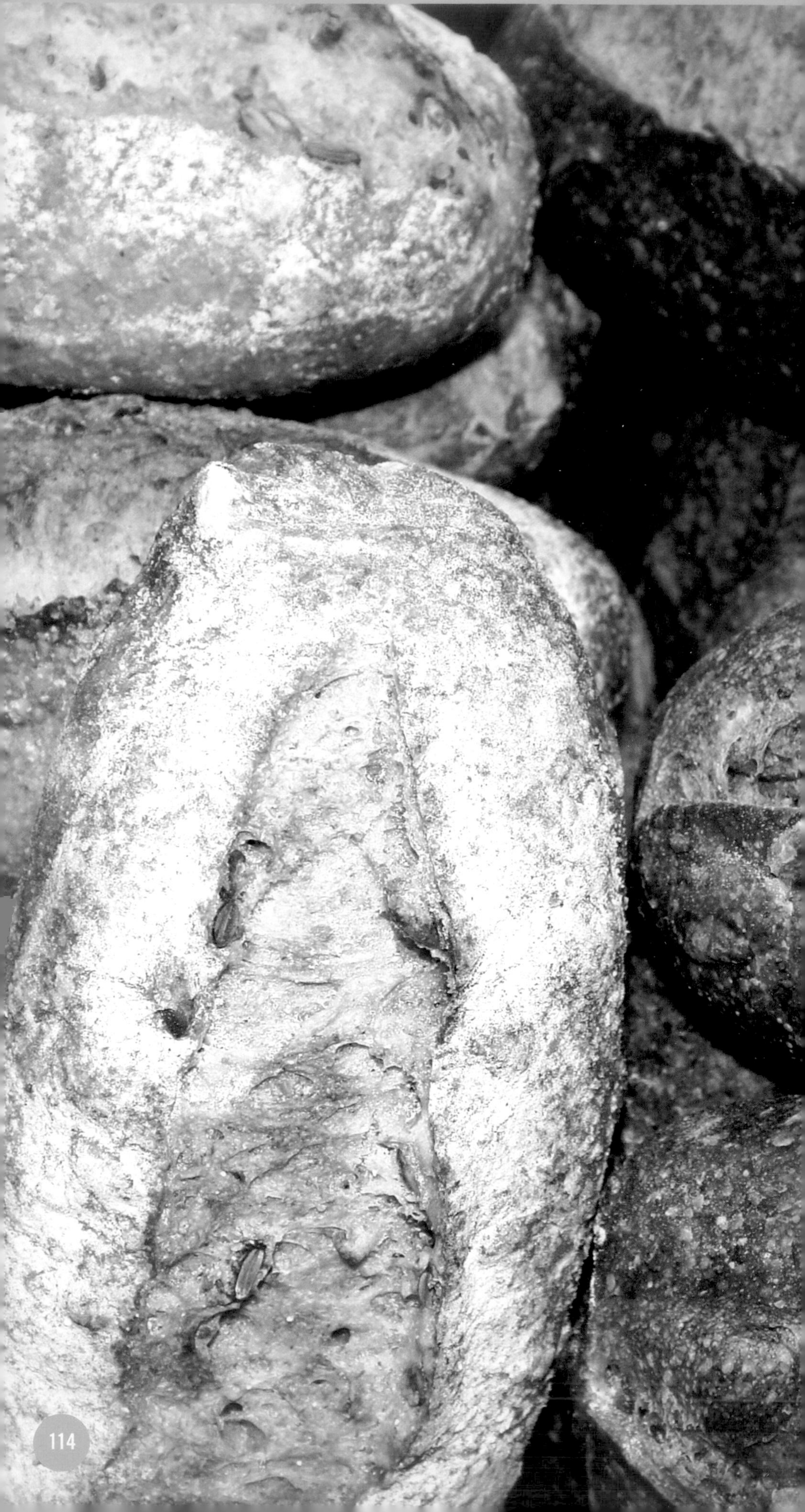

The terms "hard" and "soft" are used to describe and group different types of wheats, and refer to the texture of the kernels. Hard wheats generally have a higher protein content than soft varieties, and work particularly well in pasta. The term "durum," from the Latin for "hard," is the name given to the hardest of these wheats.

Bread Wheat

Bread wheat evolved some 8,500 years ago and is now cultivated in temperate climates all around the word. It is a "free-threshing" wheat, meaning that when it is threshed, the grain is easily separated from the rest of the plant without the need for further processing. Botanically, it has six sets of chromosomes, and so is known as a hexaploid type. Scientists believe that these extra chromosomes are partially responsible for its hardiness and the elasticity of its gluten. There are several different varieties of bread wheat particularly well suited for bread and other baked goods. This is largely on account of the quality of their gluten, which results in a dough that rises exceptionally well during baking.

Fast Fact

Free-threshing grains are those that only need to be threshed to separate the grain from the rest of the crop. Conversely, hulled grains are firmly attached to the plant inside tough, closed hulls and so additional processing is needed to release them. On one hand, free-threshing grains are less labor-intensive, but on the other, hulled grains are more protected and less susceptible to insect infestation, and so are traditionally well suited to storage.

From top: Durum wheat growing in the field; grains of durum wheat.

Durum

Durum wheat evolved from strains of emmer wheat some 8,500 years ago in parts of Europe and the Middle East. It is high in protein, including gluten, and particularly well suited for making pasta, as the protein ensures it does not become sticky or too soft on cooking.

Despite its high gluten content, durum wheat does not rise as well as bread wheat and other modern varieties. This is thought to be because even though gluten makes the dough elastic, it also makes it chewier and more firm during cooking, which can inhibit expansion.

Like all wheats, durum wheat is an excellent source of carbohydrates, fiber, and other vitamins and minerals. It has a high protein content, but does not provide a complete protein as it lacks some essential amino acids. The germ of the grain is used to produce semolina.

Fast Fact

Kansas, the main flour-milling region in the United States, produces enough wheat in one year to feed everyone in the world for two weeks.

Semolina

Semolina refers specifically to the gluten-containing endosperm of durum wheat. It is ground into various grades and used to make pasta, bread, and culinary dishes. Finely ground semolina flour is used in some pastas (generally mixed with other

Fast Fact

Cereal is named for the Roman goddess Ceres, who was said to be wheat's protector.

Pasta made from semolina

flours), while more coarsely ground semolina meal may be cooked like a gruel or risotto. The term "semolina" is also sometimes used to describe the ground endosperm of other grains such as rice or corn, but in such cases is prefaced by the name of the grain itself: for example, corn semolina and rice semolina.

Semolina is also used to make Israeli couscous and pearl couscous. About the size of a sesame seed and a large pea respectively, both are small types of pastalike preparations used in salads, as an ingredient in soups, or as accompaniments for other dishes.

Wheat Berries, Cracked Wheat, and Bulgur Wheat

These three terms refer to various types of wheat in different forms. Each comprises the whole grain and retains its nutritious bran and germ.

Wheat berries are the groats (see page 99), or raw kernels, that have had only their inedible outer shell removed. They are the least processed of these different types and so are more nutritious, but they can take three to four hours to cook.

From top: Rich semolina flour; pasta made from semolina flour; wheat berries.

Cracked wheat is raw wheat berries that have been ground into small pieces, are also nutritious, and will cook in about 20 minutes.

Bulgur (or burghul) wheat is partially boiled cracked wheat. It can be boiled in water for 10 to 15 minutes, but will also cook if placed in boiling water and left to stand, covered for about 20 minutes. It is generally used in tabboulehs and other salads in place of rice. It has a tasty, slightly nutty flavor and a chewy texture.

Fast Fact

Semolina is nutritious but rich, so a little goes a long way. One cup has more than 600 calories. Most come from carbs (approximately 82 percent), with protein contributing a further 15 percent. The remaing 3 percent comes from fat.

Left: Bulgur wheat.

Below: Tabbouleh salad made with cracked wheat, tomatoes, parsley, and onion.

Fast Fact

Some research in China indicates that wild rice may help lower cholesterol.

Wild Rice

(*Zizania aquatic* and *Zizania palustris*)

Wild rice is a grass grain but is unrelated to common or cultivated rice. Some varieties are native to the Great Lakes region of North America, whereas others are grown in Texas and Asia. The Asian variety is valued more for its greens, which are eaten as vegetables, than for its grain. Most of the wild rice sold in the United States today is farmed in California. All varieties of wild rice are semiaquatic, growing in the shallow waters of lakes and tidal rivers. This grain is difficult to grow and process, so it tends to be expensive.

Nutritional research into wild rice is in the early stages, but so far, the findings are promising. It appears that wild rice is a little higher in protein than most other grains, is a good source of various vitamins and minerals, and is lower in fat and calories than brown rice. Other research suggests that wild rice is a

Below: Uncooked and cooked wild rice.

Facing page: Chicken, vegetable, and wild rice soup.

Buying and Storing Whole Grains

Whole grains contain some oils that can be affected by heat, light, and moisture, so a little care is needed in using them.

Buying: Check that the packaging is airtight and use the "sell by" or "expiration" dates to help you choose the freshest available. If purchasing in bulk from bins, make sure the grains look fresh and don't give off a musty or oily scent.

Storing Whole-Grain Flours and Meals: Place in an airtight container labeled with the date of purchase, and then store in a cool, dry pantry or in the fridge for one month. Afterward, the container can be moved to the freezer for a couple more months. The grains may stay fresh for longer, but as the amount of oil varies, and because there is no real way of knowing how long they were stored before reaching you, it is best to use caution.

Storing Whole Grains: They will keep for up to six months in the pantry or a year in the freezer.

Storing Refined Flours and Meals: Refined flours and meals have little or no oil and can keep a little longer, but if in any doubt, apply the same guidelines as above.

When Using the Flour, Meal, or Groats: Always ensure they still look fresh and dry and emit a fresh scent. Discard if the packaging has been damaged, or if the grains, meal, or flour display any signs of damage such as a moist appearance, a musty or oily scent (even if faint), a change in color, insect infestation, mold—anything that looks suspicious. They should look and smell as fresh as when they were purchased.

FLOUR

good source of antioxidants, and might assist in lowering cholesterol. It is not a complete protein though, as it lacks certain essential amino acids.

Wild rice is usually sold as a blend with other rice, probably to make it more affordable. It is cooked in the same way as rice, at a ratio of approximately 1 cup of grains to 3 cups of water or broth that is brought to a boil, and then simmered for up to 40 minutes. It bursts when cooked, but its dark skin stays intact and it can be fluffed with a fork. It is an ideal accompaniment to other dishes or as an ingredient in salads, pilafs, and other hot rice dishes.

Fast Fact

Wild rice swells to three or four times its original size when cooked.

Rice, wild rice, and chickpeas with raisins and herbs.

Ancient Grains

The term "ancient grains" generally refers to the wheat varieties einkorn, emmer, spelt, and Kamut™. They are the biological ancestors of the wheats we eat today, which evolved through natural and cultivated crossbreeding (hybridization) over the centuries.

For the most part, these ancient wheats died out and were replaced by hardier varieties, but some remained in small pockets around the globe. In parts of Italy, for example, einkorn, emmer, and spelt have been enjoyed for centuries and are known as farro. In recent times, all these ancient wheats have attracted much interest as alternatives to modern wheats. Spelt, in particular, is now widely available.

From top: An ancient Egyptian carving shows a priest holding wheat grains; spelt berries.

A feature of many of the ancient wheat grains is that, with the exception of khorasan, they are hulled wheats, meaning the entire wheat grain is completely enclosed and attached to a tough outer husk known as a glume, which does not detach upon threshing. Therefore, after harvesting and threshing, these wheats need to be milled to detach the grain from the glume. In contrast, the glume of modern wheat varietes separates from the grain during threshing, so it does not require milling.

The need to mill three of these four ancient wheats was largely responsible for their demise during the industrial age when new machinery enabled simple, or open, threshing of the unhulled varieties.

Fast Fact

Einkorn wheat contains gluten, but some research suggests that because of its different biological structure, it may be better tolerated by people who have celiac disease or who otherwise cannot tolerate gluten.

An ancient tool used to hull wheat.

Einkorn (*Triticum monococcum*)

This ancient variety is thought to be the oldest of the wheats and was first cultivated in parts of the Middle East known as the Fertile Crescent (see page 50) more than 10,000 years ago. It has never been crossbred with any other wheat variety.

Einkorn wheat grows very tall, and its kernels are small, about a third of the size of modern varieties. So in Italy, despite its height, it is referred to as *farro piccolo*, meaning "small wheat," and it is also used as stock feed.

Einkorn wheat is higher in protein than modern wheat varieties, but like other wheats, it lacks the amino acid lysine and so is not a complete protein source. It is rich in the antioxidant beta-carotene, thought to be helpful in preventing a range of diseases, including

Turkish soup made with ancient wheats and lentils.

Einkorn grains.

certain types of cancer. It also contains the antioxidant lutein, a yellow plant pigment that is beneficial to eye health, as well as good amounts of phosphorus, potassium, and other nutrients. It contains gluten, so is not suitable for those with celiac disease.

Outside of small pockets in Europe and the Middle East, where it is often eaten in risotto-like dishes (see *farro picollo*, page 135), einkorn wheat is just beginning to reestablish itself as a food for humans, so it can be difficult to find. Consumers can find it online and in specialized natural food stores, where einkorn berries, pasta, flour, and pancake mixtures are becoming increasingly available.

Where Did They Come From?

In botanical terms, einkorn is the simplest wheat; it is a diploid species, meaning it contains two sets of chromosones. In contrast, emmer wheat and durum (which has been eaten since ancient times without significant interruption) each have four sets of chromosones and are known as tetraploid species. They evolved from the natural hybridization of einkorn wheat and a wild goatgrass, resulting in the extra chromosones. A third type of wheat includes the ancient grain spelt and the modern bread wheat that, as a result of further hybridization with wild grasses, each have six sets of chromosomes and are referred to as hexaploid species.

Emmer *(Triticum dicoccon)*

Emmer wheat is native to the Fertile Crescent and evolved at least 17,000 years ago as a natural hybridization of wild einkorn wheat and a wild goatgrass. Along with einkorn, it became one of the first cultivated wheats, probably around 8000 BC. Emmer is a hulled wheat. Its nutritional profile is similar to modern wheats, and it's a good source of carbohydrates, incomplete protein, fiber, and various vitamins and minerals. It does contain gluten, so it is not suitable for people with celiac disease.

Uncooked emmer wheat.

Fast Fact

Although not grown in as large amounts as other grains, emmer is a high-yielding crop, even in poor-quality soil. It is also resistant to certain types of fungal disease that occur in wet areas.

Farro salad with green vegetables and cheese.

Known as *farro medi* in Italy where it is readily available, emmer is usually prepared like risotto. Elsewhere, it can be purchased online or in specialty food stores in the form of berries, flour, and flakes, and with some experimentation, it can be used in baked goods such as breads and cookies, or blended with other flours.

Khorasan (*Triticum turanicum*)

Khorasan wheat is another ancient wheat that probably evolved as a hybrid of other grasses. Its exact origins are unknown, but appear to be in the Middle East. Unlike other ancient wheats, however, the grain is not enclosed within a hull.

Myths and legends abound throughout its history, including that Khorasan wheat was found in an Egyptian emperor's tomb (hence the nicknames, "King Tut's wheat"

Kamut^{TM} *wheat.*

Khorasan grains

and "pharaoh's grain"); that it was brought into Egypt by Noah on his ark (hence the name "prophet's wheat"); and that it was reintroduced into the United States in 1949 by an American airman. In Turkey, this wheat is known as "camel tooth," most likely because the grains, which are large compared to other ancient wheats, resemble the tooth of a camel.

In the United States, Khorasan wheat is grown and sold under the brand name Kamut™. Nutritionally, Khorasan wheat is higher in protein than the modern varieties, and also provides a complete protein source because it has all the essential amino acids that must be sourced through food. It is also a good source of carbohydrates, dietary fiber, vitamins, and minerals. Like other wheats, it contains gluten, so is not suitable for those with celiac disease. But Khorasan wheat provides a nutritious, high-protein alternative to wheat flour that may be better tolerated in cases of wheat sensitivity.

Khorasan wheat can be eaten whole, or used as a flour in baked goods and pasta. It has a rich, buttery flavor.

Kamut® flour.

Fast Fact

Garfagnana, a region of Italy, produces a famous pie filled with emmer or spelt, ricotta, cheese, eggs, salt, pepper, and nutmeg. Garfagnana also produces a delicious spelt soup with beans.

Spelt (*Triticum spelta*)

Spelt is related to, but quite different from, modern bread wheat varieties. It was first cultivated about 9,000 years ago in parts of Europe and the Middle East, where it remained popular for centuries before falling out of favor in the 1800s. This was most likely because its tough outer husk meant it was less suitable for processing on the newly available equipment than softer-husked grains. Recently, however, it has attracted new interest, and spelt breads, flours, and other goods are now widely available.

Spelt is highly nutritious because both the bran and the germ are retained during the milling process. It is a complete

Spelt with green beans, tomatoes, herbs, and chili.

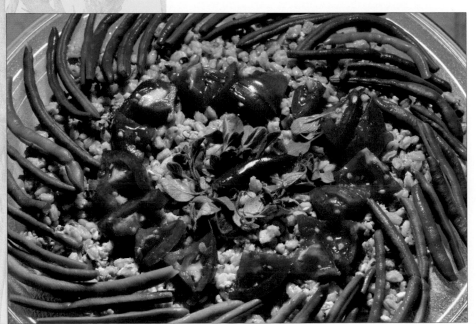

source of protein. Although it contains gluten, spelt tends to be more easily tolerated by those with certain dietary sensitivities than other wheats and is generally easily digested. It is not suitable for people with celiac disease, however.

Spelt and vegetable soup.

Like all grains, spelt is an excellent source of energy-giving carbohydrates and is also an excellent source of resistant starch (see page 33). Spelt contains a host of vitamins and minerals, including various B vitamins, manganese, and magnesium. Importantly, spelt is said to have a high degree of

Freekeh salad.

From top: Spelt in the field; spelt grains; spelt flour; spelt pasta.

bioavailability, meaning that its nutrients are readily accessed by the body.

Spelt is most commonly used as a flour (either whole-grain or refined) in bread and other baked goods in place of wheat flour. It is also available as flakes, which can be prepared as a hot cereal or used for baking in much the same way as oats. When using spelt flour instead of wheat flour in baking, it is usually necessary to reduce the amount of water added because the fiber in spelt is more water-soluble than that in wheat. The baked result will also have a slightly different texture and may rise less than if wheat flour had been used. Spelt berries, like wheat berries, comprise the entire spelt kernel and require hours of soaking and cooking before they become edible.

Farro

Farro is an Italian word that refers to the ancient grains einkorn (*farro piccolo*), emmer (*farro medio*), and spelt (*farro grande*). As implied from the descriptors *piccolo* (small), *medio* (medium), and *grande* (large), the types of farro are grouped according to grain size—but is not a strictly defining feature that the sizes of the grains in different crops can vary significantly. As a result, the term "farro" can refer to each of these three grains. In cooking, it refers to a dish where the whole wheat grain (or berry) is cooked in a similar manner as risotto. In parts of Italy in particular, farro refers specifically to emmer wheat, but in other areas, it means "a type of wheat."

Freekeh

Freekeh is green, unripened spelt that has been charred and threshed in various ways. The chaff is removed, leaving the delicious, delicately smoked and slightly sweet kernels, which do not burn due to their high moisture content. It is popular in Arabian cuisine, and very high in fiber.

Freekeh.

Pseudograins

These include various seeds that are used like cereal grains but are not defined botanically as cereal grasses because their fruits bear more than one seed. The pseudograins include quinoa, kaniwa, buckwheat, and amaranth, among others. They are currently attracting much interest as an alternative to modern cereal

grains, but most have been eaten since ancient times in various parts of the world, particularly in Africa and Asia. Unlike the ancient wheats, the popularity of pseudograins never waned between ancient and modern times, but until recently, these foods were lesser known in Western cultures. Of the pseudograins, buckwheat is probably the one that has been most familiar.

Perhaps the two main reasons for the West's interest in pseudograins, apart from the variety they add to a diet, is that many are complete sources of protein, and they are gluten-free. At the severe end of the gluten-sensitivity spectrum is celiac disease, a condition that damages the intestinal tract and restricts the absorption of nutrients. This can cause nutrient deficiencies that lead to various debilitating and potentially dangerous health disorders. Damage to the intestine can even increase the risk of bowel cancer. However, many people who have not been diagnosed with celiac disease are still sensitive to gluten and find that it does not agree with them. In all of these cases, gluten-free pseudograins offer a practical alternative.

Buckwheat.

Amaranth
(*Amaranthus caudatus*)

This pseudograin is the seed of the amaranth plant. Found by the thousands within the plant's spiky seed head, the seeds are high in protein and other nutrients. The term *amaranthus*, from the Greek, means "not to wither," and refers to the seed's hardy head.

Amaranth has been cultivated since ancient times, both for its leaves and its seeds. It was a staple of the Aztecs, who reigned through parts of North and Central America from the fourteenth to the early sixteenth centuries. The Aztecs consumed the plant in many ways: baked, toasted,

Fast Fact

Amaranth is high in protein, containing about 28 grams per cup, compared to just over 26 grams in oats, the highest in protein of the cereal grains. Amaranth also contains the amino acid lysine, and is a complete protein. Its other nutrients include iron (about 15 mg per cup), dietary fiber, and manganese.

Raw amaranth grains.

Fast Fact

Dulce de alegria, or "sweet delight," is a Mexican treat made from popped amaranth sweetened with honey or sugar. Shaped like little skulls, this treat is served during the *Día de Muertos,* or "Day of the Dead," celebrations.

Facing page: Amaranth growing.

Below: Salad made with chickpeas, amaranth, cucumber, and mint.

popped, and as tea; they even boiled the leaves and ate them as vegetables. More recently, the plant has also been widely cultivated in Africa and Asia, as a food and for ornamental purposes.

Amaranth seeds are high in protein, and contain several vitamins and minerals. They are one of the few plant sources of protein that contain all essential amino acids, and are therefore considered complete proteins.

Amaranth seeds make a valuable contribution to vegan and vegetarian diets. They are gluten-free and suitable for people with celiac disease. Preliminary research also indicates the presence of powerful phytonutrients that

may help to prevent and treat a range of conditions, including some cancers and cardiovascular and inflammatory disorders.

Amaranth seeds can be boiled in plenty of water (about six cups of water for every one cup of seeds) for about 15 minutes, before draining and serving. Amaranth is a heavy food, so it works best when combined with lighter ingredients such as leafy green vegetables and herbs. It is a suitable substitute for cracked wheat in tabbouleh, and also works well in risottos, pilafs, and salads. It has a slightly nutty, malty flavor. The seeds can also be popped to make a tasty, popcornlike snack. Ground amaranth, sometimes mixed with other flours, can be used in breads and baked goods, and as a thickener for soups, stews, and sauces. The flour is also added to some commercial breakfast cereals.

Boiled amaranth greens.

Buckwheat

(*Fagopyrum esculentum*)

Buckwheat is not a wheat or even a true grain. It is a highly nutritious pseudograin that is cultivated widely across Asia, Europe, and North America. It was first cultivated between 4000 and 5000 BC in the Balkan regions of Europe and in Japan. It moved to China around 1000 BC and spread more widely through Europe during the fourteenth and fifteenth centuries, before being introduced to the Americas and spreading around the globe.

Buckwheat is an exceptionally nutritious, gluten-free pseudograin suitable for those with celiac disease. Its many nutrients include an antioxidant known as rutin, which has been shown to

Fast Fact

Buckwheat is not related to wheat—it is a cousin of rhubarb. In their raw form, buckwheat seeds look like little triangular pebbles.

Fields of buckwheat.

help strengthen blood capillaries. As such, it helps in the treatment of conditions such as hemorrhoids and varicose veins, and it may even lower high blood pressure. Buckwheat also contains a compound known as chiroinositol that improves insulin sensitivity and can be beneficial in the treatment of type-2 diabetes. Buckwheat is a good source of carbohydrates, protein, certain B vitamins, magnesium, and iron. It is considered a complete protein. Research has also suggested a link between the consumption of buckwheat and decreased LDL ("bad") blood cholesterol levels. Its plant lignans may help protect against certain cancers and heart disease.

In North America, buckwheat is a popular ingredient in pancake and soup mixes, and in a hot cereal called kasha, which is also popular in parts of Europe and the former Soviet countries where most of the world's buckwheat crops are grown.

In Europe, it is also milled into a flour and used in various baked goods, breakfast cereals, and sweets. In Asia, buckwheat flour is mixed with wheat flour and water to make soba noodles. It has a wholesome, nutty flavor.

Facing page: Buckwheat pancakes with berry coulis.
Below: Buckwheat groats.

Fast Fact

Kaniwa
(*Chenopodium pallidicaule*)

Kaniwa is another pseudograin, nutritionally similar to quinoa (see page 149) but about half its size. It originally hails from the Andes region of South America and was an important food crop for the ancient Incan civilization.

Able to grow at very high altitudes and resistant to frost, kaniwa has survived and provided food under extreme agricultural conditions when other grains could not. It is gluten-free and high in protein and other nutrients, including iron and calcium. Kaniwa is a complete protein, and has a slightly higher protein content than quinoa.

Kaniwa is not yet established as a part of the modern Western diet, but it

Kaniwa grains.

can be found online and in specialty health stores, either in its unground form or, less commonly, as a flour that is usually mixed with other flours before being used to make baked goods. The seeds can be used in a variety of dishes, including salads, soups, and hot cereals. Kaniwa has a nutty, earthy flavor and unlike quinoa does not have the soapy-tasting coating of saponins. Kaniwa is usually boiled in water (or stock), but some chefs recommend lightly toasting the grains in a dry pan before adding the liquid—similar to the way they prepare risotto. This aids the cooking process and enhances the flavor.

Kaniwa salad with beans and corn.

Quinoa

(Chenopodium quinoa)

Quinoa (pronounced "keen-wah") is a pseudograin native to South America that was first cultivated some 7,000 years ago in the Andes Mountains of Peru. It became a dietary staple of the ancient Incan people, who called it "the mother grain."

Quinoa is a complete protein that contains significant quantities of the essential amino acid lysine, typically lacking in grains. Quinoa is also gluten-free, a good source of energy-giving, low-GI carbohydrates, and high in resistant starch. This is the starch that passes through the small intestine

Facing page: Quinoa and potato pancakes.
Below: A quinoa seed head.

Fast Fact

More than twenty years ago, scientists at NASA recommended quinoa as the perfect snack for astronauts on account of its high-protien, nutrient-rich content.

Fast Fact

Chicha is a traditional beer of the Andes, brewed from corn and quinoa.

undigested and, once in the large intestine, provides benefits similar to fiber. Quinoa is also a good source of various vitamins and minerals. Furthermore, early research suggests that certain antioxidants found in quinoa may provide significant anti-inflammatory properties.

When first harvested, quinoa has a bitter, soapy-tasting coating, comprised of saponins. This is generally washed from the seed before cooking, even though saponins are thought to have certain health benefits.

Quinoa seeds.

The seeds themselves, which come in a variety of different colors but are most commonly white, red, or brown, have a subtle, nutty flavor. Quinoa is generally cooked like rice and served as a side dish or as an ingredient in salads. Similar in size and shape to couscous, quinoa expands to about four times its original size and becomes almost translucent when cooked. An interesting feature of cooked quinoa is a small ring that forms at the edges, thought to be the germ becoming partially detached from the rest of the seed during cooking.

Fast Fact

In parts of South America, after people washed quinoa to remove the soapy-tasting saponins, the resulting rinse was often used as a shampoo.

Assorted varieties of quinoa.

The New Pseudograins

In addition to the well-established pseudograins, there are a range of other seeds that are making their way into Western diets. Many have been part of indigenous diets around the world since ancient times, but are only now beginning to gain more widespread recognition. Research into their nutritional qualities is in the early stages, but indications to date seem positive. Some of these newer pseudograins are discussed on the following pages, along with other seeds such as flax (linseed) that are long established in Western culture but appear to have greater nutritional potential than previously realized.

Above: Wattle flower (acacia).

Facing page: A quinoa plantation in Ecuador.

Fast Fact

The sap from the acacia plant is used to make gum arabic, a natural emulsifier used in the food industry. Gum arabic is also used to make a high-fiber dietary supplement to ease constipation and other digestive problems.

Acacia (*Acacia* ssp.)

This pseudograin is the edible seed of certain varieties of the acacia plant, also known as the wattle. The leaves are a common ingredient in Asian foods, where they are known as *cha om*. Acacia grows on a small, sharply thorned shrub with a distinctive and somewhat unpleasant odor that dissipates during cooking. The leaves, when cooked, have an earthy flavor and are eaten as a side dish or sometimes stirred into omelets.

The seeds of the Australian varieties of the acacia plant are a traditional food of the Australian Aboriginal people. Commercially, ground and roasted seeds are also part of the developing bushfood

Flowering acacia.

industry. They are used mainly to flavor ice cream and sauces, and sometimes they are added to baked goods. Widespread consumption remains low because the seeds are not yet common as a food outside of their traditional base. Nonetheless, they are attracting interest as a potentially nutritious food source. Nutritional information is currently limited, but early indications are that the seeds are a good source of protein, various vitamins and minerals, and low-GI carbohydrates.

Fast Fact

The ancient Egyptians used the sap of the acacia plant in their mummification process.

Acacia seeds and pods.

Chia *(Salvia hispanica)*

These ancient seeds from Mexico were a staple food of the Aztecs. They are tiny in size, either white or black.

Gluten-free and high in soluble dietary fiber, chia can help protect against bowel cancer and other disorders of the digestive tract, and is suitable for people with celiac disease. It is also high in antioxidants and omega-3 fats. Chia is often added to soups, smoothies, muesli, and various baked goods—a tablespoon can be slipped in easily to add bulk and nutrients without changing flavor. It can also be used to make a hot cereal. Chia has a high amount of protein—approximately 19 to 22 percent—and contains all the essential amino acids, making it a complete protein. Some people claim that chia can dramatically boost endurance, and this is one reason it was revered by the Aztecs.

Hot cereal made with white chia and served with berries.

Soaked chia seeds can be used in place of flour to thicken sauces and soups. Chia flour is available too, and can be used in baking, but it is best to mix it with other flours in a ratio of about one part chia to three parts flour.

One curious feature of chia is that when it is immersed in liquid, it forms a viscous gel—mucilage—around its perimeter. This is soluble fiber and it enables the seed to absorb up to twelve times its weight in water. In turn, this greatly assists satiety and hydration.

Black chia seeds.

Fast Fact

Chia is an ancient Mayan word that means "strength."

Above left: Yogurt with fruit and chia seeds.

Left: Sprouted chia and seeds.

Fast Fact

The linseed oil sold in paint stores comes from the same seed and plant as flaxseeds, but it has been chemically processed. It is highly toxic, flammable, and dangerous if not handled correctly.

Flaxseed (*Linum usitatissimum*)

Flaxseeds, also known as linseeds, are small, dark brown seeds a little larger than sesame seeds. Their greatest claim to fame is that, along with chia, they are one of the richest plant sources of omega-3 fats, which help reduce blood cholesterol. Along with other nutrients, flaxseeds also contain lignans, which act like the female hormone estrogen and are thought to help ease some of the discomforts of menopause. Lignans may also have certain anticancer properties.

Adding a tablespoon or two of flaxseed to foods such as breakfast cereals, smoothies, soups, and casseroles is a way to add fiber and bulk while boosting

Cookies made with flaxseed flour.

omega-3 intake. A popular supplement called LSA is a blend of ground flaxseeds, almonds, and sunflower kernels.

Finely ground flaxseed can be used as a flour or meal in baked goods or pancakes, but it is generally mixed with some other flour, as it is quite heavy.

Flaxseed flowers.

Flaxseeds and flaxseed flour are high in fat, and neither has a very long shelf life. Both should be stored in airtight containers in the fridge, where the seeds should stay fresh for up to twelve months and the flour will keep for up to two months. Always be guided by the information on the package, however, because storage times depend in part on how fresh the seeds and flour were to begin with. Because flaxseed flour does not keep for long, some people prefer to purchase only the seeds and grind them into flour as needed.

Flaxseeds.

White Goosefoot

(*Chenopodium album*)

This plant goes by various names, including lamb's quarters, pig weed, and wild spinach. It fosters mixed responses: some people consider it a weed, but others protest its culinary uses. It is closely related to quinoa (see page 149).

As a food, white goosefoot is probably best known as a green vegetable, but its seeds are high in protein and can be used to make flour. It is grown in northern India, and outside of this region, the seeds are not readily available. So their possible use in foods is little known or understood.

Fast Fact

When eaten as a green vegetable, white goosefoot is said to be more nutritious than spinach.

Above: Lamb's quarters.

Facing page: Flowering white goosefoot.

Flour Alternatives

Not that long ago, people with celiac disease or other dietary conditions that prevented them from eating wheat products were restricted to eating a limited array of foods just to avoid the gluten. Not so today. Flours made from gluten-free cereal grains such as oats or corn, and from pseudograins like buckwheat, are now widely available. There's also a wide range of foods made from nuts, beans, and other plant sources such as potatoes. Each brings its own character and quality to the foods in which it is used.

Foods made from nuts will have a high fat content. As a result, they will spoil easily and have a shorter shelf life. Nut-based foods should be stored in airtight containers in the fridge for short periods only. The storage life of these flours

Almonds with almond flour.

varies depending on the nuts used and other factors, so always review their packaging.

Gluten-free flours result in heavier, denser baked goods because it is gluten that enables dough to stretch. This leads to a lighter finish. However, leavening agents can be added to gluten-free flours to compensate for the lack of gluten. Leavening agents include baking soda, baking powder, and yeast, among others.

Cautions:

Nuts: Tree nuts—and any flours made from them, including acorn flour and almond flour—are the second most common form of food allergies after peanuts. People with nut allergies should not be exposed to or eat nut flours. Some other flours, including arrowroot flour, are also known to provoke allergic reactions, although that is less common. All foods have the potential to cause allergic reactions in people with particular sensitivities, so awareness and care is always required in this area.

Gluten: When produced correctly, alternative flours should be free of gluten, but it is wise to always check the packaging for any added ingredients that may introduce gluten or other allergens.

Here are a few alternative flours to consider:

Acorn Flour

Made from the nutrient-rich nuts of oak trees, acorn flour is a good source of protein, carbohydrates, fats, fiber, and various minerals.

Almond Flour

This flour—made from ground, blanched, or whole almonds—has a strong but appealing nutty flavor. In addition, almond meal adds a grainy texture to foods in which it is used. Almond flour is popular in some almond-flavored cakes and cookies, especially in Italy. Similar in appearance to cornstarch, almond flour is used primarily as a thickener.

Chestnut Flour

Popular in Italy, this delicious flour has a strong yet mellow, almost sweet flavor. It is used in baked goods and as a thickener. Although it has less fat and more carbohydrates than other nut flours, chestnut must be stored in the fridge for short periods only. An unusual flour, it lends itself to sweet, slightly earthy cakes as well as savory dishes.

Almond flour.

Chickpea Flour

Made from raw or roasted chickpeas (garbanzo beans), chickpea flour is gluten-free, high in protein, and suitable for people with nut allergies. It is popular in Indian cuisine, where it is used to make batters for pakora (a type of fried snack), as well as being used as a thickener and in baked goods. The raw flour has a slightly bitter flavor.

Pancakes made with chickpea flour.

Coconut Flour

Made from finely ground dried coconut meat with the fat removed, this high-fiber, gluten-free, low-carb flour is similar in texture to wheat flour and has a slightly sweet taste.

Pea Flour

Made from roasted and ground yellow field peas, this flour ranges from smooth to gritty and has a strong, earthy flavor. It is high in fiber and is also quite starchy, but also offers some protein.

Plantain Flour

This flour is made from the plantain, a fruit that is similar to a banana. It is high in carbohydrates and low in fat, but fairly dense in calories—only a little less dense than all-purpose flour.

Potato Flour

This is made from cooked and dried potatoes that are ground into a fine flour with a texture similar to wheat flour. Potato flour behaves differently during baking, though, leading to a heavier, denser, and sometimes more moist result. It is also used as a thickener. It has a short shelf life, but some manufacturers add preservatives to lengthen that.

Potato flour.

Soy Flour

This is made from ground soybeans, the "complete protein bean" that is so nutritious it is used to make some soy milks and other soy products. The taste and texture vary depending on the manufacturer, but overall soy flour has a smooth texture and mild flavor.

Tapioca Flour

Sometimes called cassava flour, this is a smooth, starchy flour produced from the roots of the South American cassava plant. Tapioca flour is used in baked goods and as a thickener, and its slightly sweet flavor is barely discernible. It is often used in combination with other flours, and to make a delicious sweet Brazilian crepe, also known as tapioca.

The Brazilian sweet treat, tapioca.

Let's Talk About Beans

Legumes, Beans, Pulses, and Peas

Are legumes, beans, pulses, and peas the same thing? Confusingly, these terms are often used interchangeably, but they also have their own meanings that change and overlap across different countries and cultures. One person's pulse, therefore, can be another's bean.

Here, "bean" refers to the nutritious fruit, or part of the fruit such as the pod or the seed, of various bean plants (also known as legumes). "Dry beans" refers to the dried seeds of these plants (also known as pulses). These include lentils, kidney beans, lima beans, split peas, mung beans, and various others. Finally, "fresh beans" and "fresh peas" refer to the pods and seeds of beans that are eaten as fresh vegetables rather than dried before being cooked. It should be noted that the terms "beans" and "peas" sometimes also appear as part of a dry bean's common name, such as black-eyed pea, chickpea (garbanzo), and lima bean.

Facing page: Minestrone.

There are other types of legumes as well. These include forage legumes (alfalfa), nutlike legumes (peanuts), fruit legumes (tamarind), soy, and carob.

The names and uses sometimes get confusing, but for the purposes of this book, this section is intended as a general introduction. It should provide some insight into the nutritional, economic, and ecological value of the humble bean in all its forms.

Where Do Beans Come From?

Many beans were first cultivated in the Middle East some 10,000 years ago. Others have their origins in ancient Central and South America. Globally, they have been a staple food for thousands of years—second only to grains. Although they vary in size, shape, and color, their common feature is that the plant's seeds are enclosed in pods that split into two halves.

Beans are an excellent source of plant-based protein. Almost all beans are, however, incomplete proteins in that they do not contain all of the essential amino acids that the body cannot make on its own.

Hummus, an Middle Eastern dip made from beans.

This is easily rectified if beans are paired with a complementary food containing the missing amino acids. Grains are an excellent choice for this purpose. Cultures around the globe have understood the benefits of the bean—grain mix for centuries, as can be seen in many traditional dishes, including the minestrones of Italy, the burritos of South America, the stir-fries of Asia, and the hearty stews of Africa.

The relative affordability of beans in comparison to more expensive meat protein has also contributed to their enduring popularity. But beans offer more than just affordable protein: They are also a great source of fiber, low-GI carbohydrates, vitamins, minerals, and antioxidant phytonutrients. Most are also low in fat, though peanuts and soybeans are exceptions. Beans are also thought to promote good health by helping to reduce the risk of certain chronic diseases, including diabetes, obesity, and cancer.

Beans and Nitrogen

Most bean plants (legumes) are nitrogen-fixing plants. Nitrogen is essential for the life and growth of both animals and plants, but despite its abundance in the

Fast Fact

Beans provide niacin, thiamin, riboflavin, vitamin B6, calcium, and iron. They are rich in complex carbohydrates, protein, fiber, and potassium—one cup has more potassium than a banana. Beans are the best source of folate, and are low in fat and free of saturated fat, trans fats, and cholesterol.

soil and atmosphere, it most often appears in a form that animals and plants cannot use. A bacteria called rhizobia lives in the roots of bean plants and converts nitrogen from the atmosphere into something called fixed nitrogen. Fixed nitrogen is used by the plant itself, but is also released into the soil where it becomes available to other plants. In turn, animals obtain their nitrogen either by eating plants containing fixed nitrogen, or by eating animals that ate those plants.

Because they are nitrogen-fixing, legumes are sometimes also called green manure. Many traditional farming cultures have alternated between leguminous and non-leguminous crops for centuries, turning the mature plants into the soil at

Turning green manure into the soil.

the end of a season, so they can decompose and release nitrogen into the soil. This helps to restore the health of the soil between plantings.

How Much Is a Serving?

One serving of cooked beans is about half a cup, with the exception of peanuts and soybeans. A serving of peanuts is equal to one ounce. A serving of a soybean food varies depending on its other ingredients and the method of production, so it is necessary to check the label on the package. Generally, typical servings of tofu and tempeh are approximately 5⅓ ounces and 4 ounces, respectively.

Fast Fact

The U.S. Department of Agriculture recommends that adults eat at least three cups of beans each week.

Dry Beans

Dry beans, also known as pulses, are the dried seeds of the bean fruit. They include split peas, chickpeas, lentils, and kidney beans, among others. They come in a range of colors, shapes, and sizes, peeled or unpeeled, sometimes split and sometimes not. Most (with the exception of small lentils) need to be soaked before cooking; soaking and cooking rehydrates the beans. In some cases, the soaking is essential because it removes toxins; in others, it is an important step that helps make the dry beans more digestible and certain nutrients in them more available to the human body.

Dry beans are typically used in stews, casseroles, soups, dips, bean pastes, and a wide range of other foods. Some are ground into a flour and used in baking, as a thickener in sauces and stews, and to make batter for pakoras and other fried dishes. Dry beans can be stored for several months, so they have long been a valuable winter food source. Canned dry beans, available at supermarkets, have already been soaked and cooked, making them a convenient way to incorporate beans into your diet. (Be sure to check the labels and choose those with no added salt or sugar.) Many people believe, however, that home-soaked dry beans hold their shape, texture, nutrients, and sometimes their colors and patterns better than those that are canned. Opinions vary, but whether they are soaked at home or canned, all dry beans are worthy additions to a healthy diet.

Another nice thing about dry beans is that many are available in a delightful array of cheerful colors and patterns. Like colorful little buttons, they exude a sense of happiness and contentment, and somehow take on their own distinct personalities. For example, navy beans have a certain nautical feel, appaloosas have markings similar to horses, and tongue-of-fire beans are lashed with vibrant "flames." So it is not surprising that beautiful dry bean

Fast Facts

Bean benefits:

- They're low-fat, cholesterol-free, and high-fiber, and may reduce the risk of heart disease.
- Beans are a natural source of antioxidants and phytochemicals that may reduce the risk of certain cancers.
- They have a low glycemic index, which helps keep blood sugar in the normal range.
- Beans are great for growth and energy. Their protein helps build, repair, and maintain muscle, while their carbs provide a sustained energy source.

collections are often stored in glass jars and then placed on display to show off their colors and patterns. In most cases, these colors and patterns disappear during the cooking process, but not always.

Storing Dry Beans

Dry beans should be stored in airtight containers and kept in a cool, dry place out of direct sunlight. Although they may keep for a year or more if stored correctly, it is generally better to use them within six months of purchase. Dry beans that have lost their freshness will begin to fade in color and lose their subtle sheen. They may also start to show other flaws, such as cracked or broken seed coats. Stale dry beans are unlikely to soften properly on soaking and cooking.

Sorting and Soaking

All dry beans except lentils and split peas should be soaked before they are cooked. Most should be left to soak for as long as possible (generally overnight, for at least eight hours, and up to twelve hours for large ones). Mung beans and navy beans may need only four or five hours.

Soaking times will also vary depending on factors such as the weather and even the hardness of the water. Soaking makes the rehydrated dry beans more digestible, shortens the cooking time, and removes toxins. It also helps break down the compounds that cause flatulence.

Before soaking, remove small stones, shriveled or odd-looking dry beans, and any other debris. This is known as sorting. After sorting, many people recommend rinsing the dry beans, but others say this causes the beans to rehydrate too soon and is unnecessary because they will be rinsed again later. For the most part, though, a quick rinse in cold water is unlikely to harm them and is a good precautionary measure.

After rinsing, cover the beans in lots of fresh, cold water (about

Fast Facts

Bean benefits, continued:

- Their high fiber content promotes satiety and can assist in weight loss and management.

- They are a great source of folate, which women need in higher quantities during pregnancy.

Soaking chickpeas in water.

four times the volume of the beans themselves) and leave them to soak. In hot weather, soak them in the refrigerator to prevent fermentation. Dry beans are likely to wrinkle as they begin to rehydrate, but by the time they are fully rehydrated, they will have at least doubled in size and should be plump and smooth. When they are ready, rinse them thoroughly in preparation for boiling.

A quicker method entails boiling the dry beans in plenty of water for about three minutes and then allowing them to stand for at least four hours. Discard the water, rinse the beans in cold water, and then boil.

Never use the same water for cooking that the dry beans were soaked in.

Cooking Dry Beans

Place the dry beans in a saucepan with plenty of water, bring them to a boil, and cook until they are tender. Cooking times will vary depending on the size of the beans and other factors, such as the prior soaking time and even the weather, but it can be anywhere from 20 to 90 minutes or more. Stir them occasionally as they boil, and top up with extra water if too much is lost during the boiling process. The beans should be covered in water at all times. Some people like to salt the beans as they cook, but wait until they are soft. Adding salt too early is likely to result in tough skins and overly firm beans. A tablespoon of vegetable oil added to the

boiling pot may reduce foaming and keep the pot from boiling over. Every now and then, carefully remove a few beans from the pot with a spoon, allow them to cool, and

Boiling beans.

bite into them to see if more time is required. Test a few to ensure a consistent texture throughout the batch.

Using a Pressure Cooker

Some people like to cook their dry beans in a pressure cooker because it is quicker—but not that much quicker because, with the exception of lentils and split peas, the beans still need to be soaked. The most important reason for soaking is to remove toxins that are present in some unsoaked beans. Once the beans have been soaked, their cooking time can be reduced to just a few minutes in a pressure cooker.

Because equipment varies, as does the quality of the dry beans, it is important that you consult the manufacturer's instructions for using the pressure cooker. With that in mind, here are the basic steps. In most cases, this will make 5 to 6 cups of beans.

First, soak one pound of dry beans in water overnight (see pages 176–78). The next morning, rinse and drain them. Place them in the pressure cooker, then cover with 8 cups of water. Add 1 teaspoon of salt, plus flavorings such as onion, garlic, and a few herbs such as a bay leaf or two. Add 1 tablespoon of vegetable oil; this is important because it will help to prevent foaming, which can cause blockages in the pressure valve. Next, secure the lid according to the manufacturer's instructions.

Place the cooker on the stove on high heat until it reaches high pressure, then reduce to medium or medium-low heat. (If you are using an electric pressure

A pressure cooker can cook beans quickly.

cooker, you will need to consult the manufacturer's manual and adapt the process as required.)

Once the heat has been reduced, set a timer and let the beans cook. The cooking time varies depending on the size and type of bean and other factors, so some experimentation may be required. Consult the manual for guidance on cooking times, but if it does not provide this information, a good starting point is 15 minutes on high, and another 10 minutes on reduced heat, followed by cooling and depressurizing time. (If you find that the beans are not cooked enough, you can finish them off on the stove and allow more time next time.)

Once the cooking time has elapsed, allow the pot to cool down and depressurize. Follow the manufacturer's instructions on how to depressurize your cooker, and how to determine when it will be ready to be opened. Once ready, unlock the lid and carefully remove it, tilting it away from you to protect your face and body from the steam. Remove bay leaves and any large added ingredients, such as onion and garlic, with a slotted spoon and discard. The beans and broth are now ready to use.

Storing Cooked Beans

Do not store beans in their original cooking pot. Instead, after cooking, drain and cool the beans, and then put them in airtight containers and cover them with liquid—many people use the bean broth left in the pot after cooking because it is so flavorful. Seal the container and place it in the fridge. The beans will keep for three or four days. They will last for six months or more in the freezer. Make sure you label the container with the date the beans were cooked. Don't leave the cooked beans at room temperature for more than an hour because this can cause bacteria to multiply. If at any time, the beans emit an unpleasant odor or appear to have changed their appearance, don't eat them. They have spoiled.

Chickpeas (*Cicer arietinum*)

Chickpeas are nutritionally similar to common beans, but are higher in calcium and lower in potassium. They originated in the Middle East at least 7,000 years ago before spreading to the Mediterranean region and then into Africa, India, and the Americas. In the United States they are generally called garbanzo beans. They were a popular food among the ancient Greeks, Romans, and Egyptians, and today are found all around the world as an exceptionally nutritious and versatile food. Other common names include Bengal grams and Egyptian peas. Their Latin name, *Cicer arietinum*, means "small ram" and is a reference to the bean's unusual and irregular shape, thought to resemble the head of a ram. Chickpeas have a mild nutty flavor and a smooth yet starchy texture that turns crumbly upon eating. The two most popular types of chickpea are the kabuli and desi.

Fast Fact

Chickpeas have long been used in folk medicine. Fluids extracted from the stems, leaves, and pods contain compounds that are said to have aphrodisiac properties and also to help treat bronchitis, constipation, diarrhea, flatulence, warts, and various other disorders.

Spanish chickpeas in a stew with ham.

Fast Fact

Chickpea flour, also known as besan flour, is used in gluten-free flatbreads, to make the batter for pakoras, and as a thickener in sauces and curries. It should be made from cooked chickpeas rather than ground raw beans.

Desi

The desi chickpea is widely consumed in India and parts of the Middle East, where it is used in various everyday dishes, including hummus, falafel, curries, and dal. They are about half the size of the kabuli, and are dark brown or black in color. They are also known by various other names, including Bengal gram. The chana dal (see page 222) is a desi type of chickpea without its seed coat.

Chickpea hummus served with flatbread.

Kabuli

Kabuli chickpeas are a pale cream color and round in shape. These are the most commonly eaten chickpea in the United States. As the name suggests, this type is thought to have come from Kabul, Afghanistan, and today is grown all over the world.

Other Varieties

Other chickpea varieties include Bombay chickpeas, which are slightly larger than the desi type. The unusual ceci neri, or black chickpea, of southern Italy is also larger than the desi, and significantly darker.

From top: Kabuli chickpeas with besan flour; falafel made with chickpeas

Chickpeas are sometimes fermented, especially in some Middle Eastern dishes including hummus. Fermented foods offer particular health benefits in that they contain probiotics ("good" bacteria) that support bowel health and the absorption of nutrients, and they also keep longer than unfermented foods. The process of fermenting foods is, however, specialized, and should not be undertaken without the requisite knowledge.

Ceci neri.

Fast Fact

North Dakota is the top U.S. bean-growing state, followed by Michigan, Nebraska, and Minnesota.

Common Beans
(*Phaseolus vulgaris*)

Many dry beans fall into the botanical group *Phaseolus vulgaris,* meaning common ("vulgar") bean. Hence they are known generally as "common beans." They originated in Central and South America at least 8,000 years ago and are now grown all around the world. They also include some modern varieties that have been cultivated in Europe and elsewhere. Some common beans grow on bushes, while others climb on poles and trellises. Dry common beans include many everyday beans such anasazi, borlotti, and great northern, as well as some exotic varieties. All common beans are good sources of iron, potassium, selenium, molybdenum, and various B vitamins, especially folate. Some are also eaten as fresh green vegetables (see page 254).

A selection of common beans.

Anasazi

This small, ancient, kidney-shaped bean gets it name from the Anasazi Indians who lived in the Four Corners region of the United States (Utah, Arizona, Colorado, and New Mexico) and were probably the first people to cultivate it. After centuries of neglect, the bean has gradually reestablished itself in contemporary diets since the mid-1950s. Speculation surrounds its revival, including tales of ancient pots of seeds being found in archaeological digs, from which new plants sprouted. But a more plausible explanation is that it stayed in cultivation in gardens nurtured by Native Americans before being "discovered" and sold in the general population. Predominantly white in color, it is covered with maroon splotches. It is sweet in flavor, has a creamy texture, and has fewer gas-producing properties than other beans. It swells to about three times its size after soaking, and cooks quickly. It is also known as the Aztec bean, New Mexico appaloosa bean, Jacob's cattle bean, and New Mexico cave bean.

Anasazi beans.

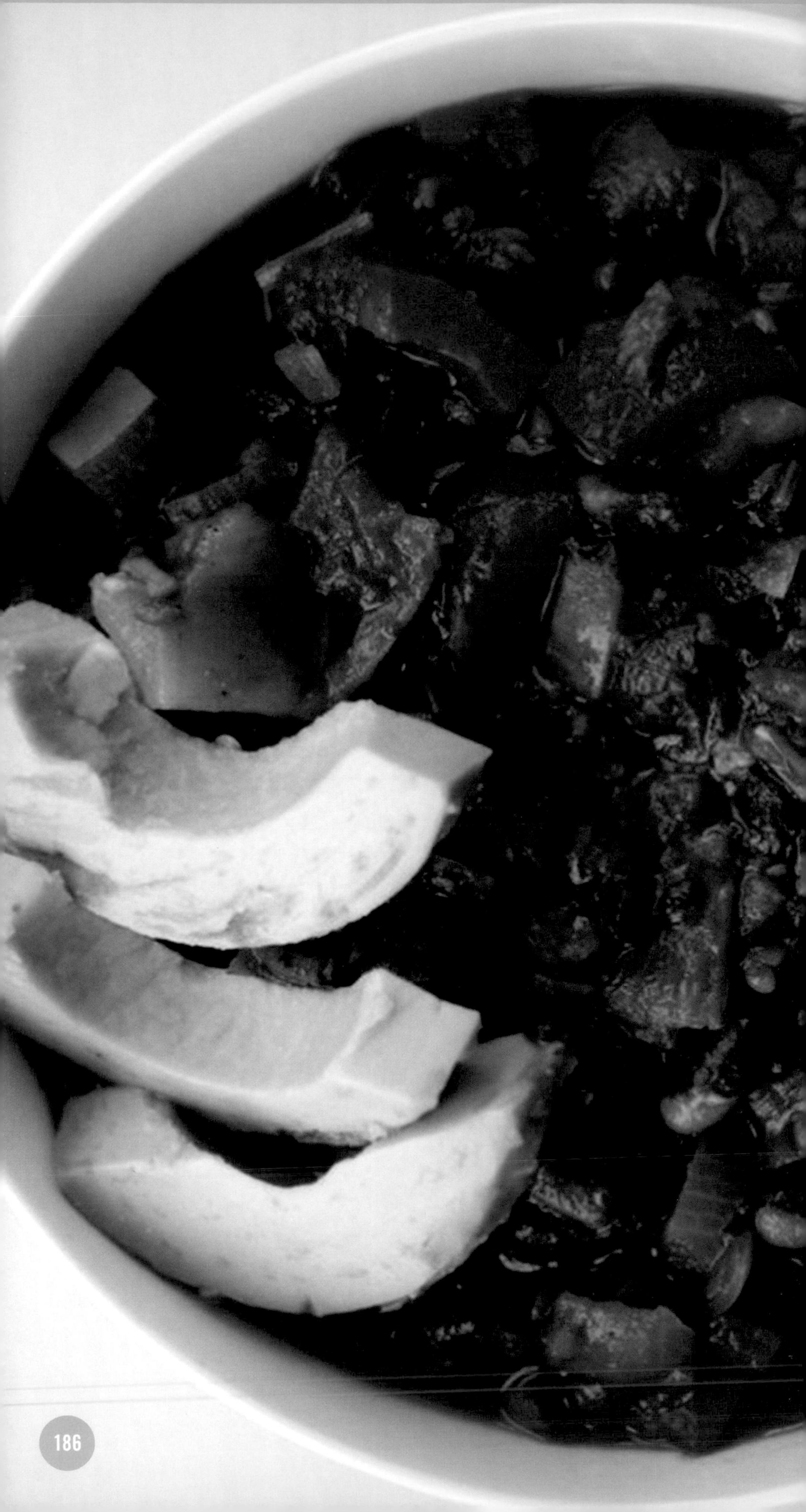

Appaloosa

While bearing similar markings to the anasazi, this is a different variety. It is slightly curved rather than kidney shaped and is a bit longer. Its base color is ivory, and it is largely covered in dark purple (sometimes nearly black) markings. The bean is named for these markings, which resemble those of Appaloosa horses.

Originally from the Palouse area of New Mexico, this bean has an earthy flavor and a firm texture, even after soaking and cooking. It retains its shape well on cooking and, like many other dry beans, is ideal for a range of savory dishes including soups, stews, and chilis. The pods of young appaloosas are also sometimes eaten as green vegetables.

Fast Fact

The appaloosa broth (the water in which the beans have been cooked) is known as pot liquor, or *caldo de frijol*, in South America and makes a great base for soups and sauces.

Facing page: Appaloosa chili.
Below: Appaloosa beans.

Natural Gas

Digestive wind is part of the digestive process, but certain foods increase the amount, causing bloating and flatulence. Dry beans are notorious offenders. This intestinal gas is produced by bacteria in the gut as they break down food. For the most part, it is composed of methane, hydrogen, and carbon dioxide, and for some reason, some people produce more methane than others.

Some foods are more difficult to digest than others, such as beans, bran, seeds, and vegetables such as cauliflower, onion, and cabbage. These foods move from the small intestine to the bowel (large intestine) before being properly digested. Then they are broken down in the bowel, resulting in increased flatulence. Other factors such as stress or intolerance to certain foods can also cause food to pass to the bowel too quickly, further contributing to flatulence.

Flatulence is largely the result of the body processing less digestible foods in the bowel, but processes such as steaming, soaking, and cooking will make the foods more digestible and less likely to produce gas. This needs to be balanced, however, with the need to preserve nutrients (which overprocessing and removing fiber can destroy).

Marrowfat beans are notorious for causing flatulence.

Flatulence is not unhealthy and is only a problem if it causes discomfort or other issues. It also seems that when people eat less digestible foods regularly, the body may adapt, at least partially. For example, when people first embark on a high-fiber diet, they may find they produce more gas, but this tends to settle after a few days.

Many people believe that a good way to make dry beans more digestible is to soak them overnight. In severe cases, and under medical supervision, people may take manufactured enzymes to assist the digestive process when they eat such foods.

John Bull directs gas at a poster of George III
Richard Newton (1777–98)

Black Turtle

This is a tasty little dry bean, about the size of a pea, and jet black in color with a creamy flesh within. The texture is soft, and the flavor sweet and earthy. Black turtle beans are especially popular in South America and the Caribbean, and are known by various other names, including Venezuelan beans, Tampico beans, and turtle soup beans. They are grown in the warm months and are left on the plant to dry. Once harvested, the plants themselves are left in the field as green manure, on account of their nitrogen-fixing properties (see pages 171–72).

Fast Fact

Like the broth of the appaloosa bean, black turtle bean broth (*caldo de frijol*) is used as a nutritious and tasty base for various soups and sauces.

Facing page: Chili con carne.

Borlotti and spelt soup.

Fast Fact

Although the borlotti is thought to be a classic Italian bean of South American origin, it is also known as the cranberry bean in the United States, where it is produced in high volumes—and exported to Italy and sold as borlottis.

Facing page: Roman-style minestrone.

Borlotti

Originating from Colombia, where they are known as *cargamento*, borlottis are pinkish-cream and have darker pink or crimson speckles when they are raw, but become completely brown when cooked. The pod is also deep pink and cream in color. These dry beans are medium-to-large in size with a sweet, slightly nutty flavor and a creamy texture. They are used extensively in Italian and Portuguese cuisine. In Italy, they are also known as the romano, and elsewhere they are the cranberry bean. They are especially high in protein, yielding approximately 17 grams per cup, and high in potassium. Cooked with onions and tomatoes, they make a delicious side dish and are the perfect bean for a hearty minestrone.

Calypso

Although calypsos come in different colors, perhaps the most celebrated is the black calypso bean, an heirloom variety also known as *yin yang* or *orca*, which displays a beautiful black-and-white (and sometimes red-and-white) pattern. This dry bean comes from the Caribbean, it has a nutty flavor with hints of onion, and its flesh is generally creamy, like that of creamed potatoes. Calypsos are valued for their nutrition, but they are also popular, after harvesting, as green manure. They are one of the best for baking and soups, and are frequently paired with flavorful ingredients such as ham hocks or garlic.

Fast Fact

One of the most divine features of this dry bean is purely aesthetic: These exquisite, jewel-like beans (often hard to find, unfortunately) hold both their shape and pattern when cooked. The pattern may fade slightly, but is still there.

Facing page: Stew made with calypsos and corn.

Cannellini

Cannellini's other names include Italian white bean and fasolia bean. They were first grown in Argentina by Italian immigrants and later taken back to Italy, where they became an everyday food. As well as being a good source of protein, low-GI carbohydrates, and dietary fiber, cannellini beans are high in antioxidants and are a significant source of calcium. They are also high in the trace mineral molybdenum, which plays a role in the body's detoxification.

Cannellinis are a favorite in Tuscany, where they are eaten warm as a side dish, mixed into salads and soups, and even combined with pasta. Creamy in color and texture, they have a mild, slightly nutty flavor. They are also firm, and hold their

Cannellini bean and vegetable soup.

Fast Fact

Pureed and warmed cannellini beans are a great alternative to mashed potatoes: creamy, delicious, high in fiber and protein, and without all the high-GI carbs.

shape well when cooked. Many cannellini recipes are centuries old, but today we also use cannellinis as a base for dips instead of high-fat cream cheeses and oils, or add a tablespoon or two to a smoothie to give it a creamy protein boost.

Below: Cannellini bean salad with cherry tomatoes, chorizo, and red onion.

Flageolet

Flageolets were first grown in France in the nineteenth century and are traditionally served with lamb. They are small, immature, and delicate, and the seeds come in a variety of colors, including white, black, and pale green. Like many other small beans, they are often used as a substitute for the tarbais bean, the preferred bean for the traditional slow-cooked French cassoulet.

Flageolets are often confused with French navy beans, and the terms are often used interchangeably. However, flageolets are a specific French variety. French navy

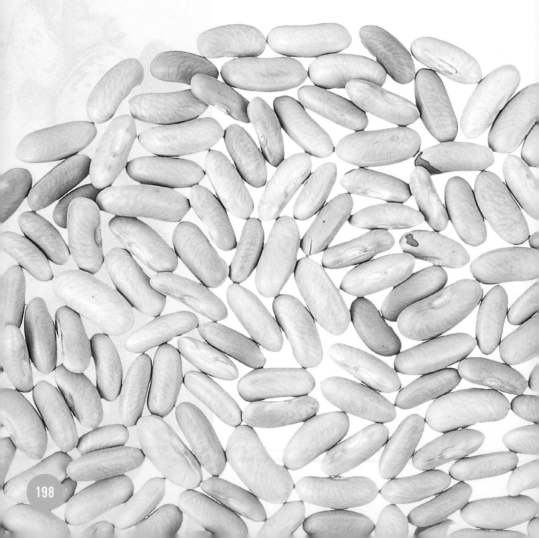

Fast Fact

Flageolet pods are inedible.

Cooked flageolets.

beans, on the other hand, are most likely white beans of American origin that found their way to Europe in the sixteenth century.

In France, the flageolet is often described by the color of its seeds: flageolet noir for black, flageolet rouge for red, and flageolet jaune for yellow. One variety, flageolet vert, has what appears to be green seeds but is actually a white-seeded variety with the ability to retain chlorophyll under certain conditions, making them appear to be green.

Fast Fact

Great northern beans are not large, as their name might suggest. Rather, they are a small dry bean with a delicate appearance. They are a favorite in the United States, largely due to their smooth texture and mild flavor.

Great Northern

This small white or pale cream dry bean is so called because it hails from Canada and the northern regions of the United States, including North Dakota and Minnesota, where it grows naturally and is cultivated. It can also be eaten fresh. The beans have a neutral flavor, so they are often added to casseroles and soups to plump them up without altering flavor. Great northerns are also sometimes used to soak up excess fluids, to prevent stews from becoming too "soupy," or to help bind other ingredients.

Great northerns have a smooth texture, and they hold their shape well after boiling. Although most commonly used in savory dishes, they are also suitable for sweeter dishes, due to their neutral flavor.

The beans are most commonly used in soups, stews, and casseroles but also make a simple, satisfying side dish if warmed and served with butter or olive oil and spices. Sometimes they are whipped to make a hummus like dip, or added to recipes for bread and other baked goods. Great northerns are also a good substitute for other white beans such as cannellini or flageolets, if needed. Like all dry beans, they are a nutritious source of plant protein. In particular, they are noted for their calcium content.

Salad made with great northern beans, chickpeas, and black-eyed peas.

Fast Fact

One cup of cooked kidney beans has only 225 calories, most of which (about 70 percent) comes from the carbohydrates. The protein content is about 26 percent, and the remainder is fats.

Kidney Beans

This dry bean originated in Mexico in ancient times and was an important food for the Aztec people. It then spread through South and Central America, and later into Europe, Africa, and Asia.

Fresh kidney beans are so named because of their kidneylike shape. The raw beans are not edible and contain a toxic substance known as phytohemagglutinin. Although this chemical is found in many beans, it is particularly high in kidney beans. Therefore, kidney beans must mature on the plant until they are dry, and then be soaked and boiled before consumption. Once cooked, they display a deep red color, and hold their shape well.

Like other dry beans, they are an excellent source of plant protein, yielding about 15 grams per cup. They are also high

in dietary fiber, folate, and various other vitamins and minerals. They are particularly high in molybdenum, which has an important role in detoxification.

Kidney beans are a popular addition to many savory dishes, including casseroles and hearty, Mexican-style chilis. They are also served cold in salads, or warm drizzled with olive oil and spices.

Fast Fact

The fact that kidney beans absorb the flavors of other foods makes them particularly well suited for chili.

Chili con carne made with kidney beans.

Fast Fact

Marrow beans were originally a rare bush bean that first became popular in the mid-1800s. Although the beans were used primarily in baking, and appreciated for their slightly meaty flavor, the young pods were often shelled, and the seeds within eaten as a fresh vegetable.

Marrow Beans

These large, plump, whitish dry beans look like oversized navy beans, sometimes with a toothlike or pebblelike appearance. Especially popular in Middle Eastern and Italian cuisines, they were also popular in North America in the nineteenth century and remain a favorite in baked bean dishes today. With a strong flavor that is often compared to bacon, they work well served on their own or in soups, stews, and other dishes. They have long been called marrowfat beans because of their rich, meaty flavor and texture, but recently this somewhat unappealing name has largely given way to marrow bean. Losing the "fat" has given them a healthier, greener image.

Marrow beans need lengthy soaking and should be cooked until they are soft, especially because they are notorious for producing flatulence when eaten undercooked. When in season, young marrow beans can also be eaten fresh, or they can be cooked in less time than older beans require. The fresh beans tend to have a creamier texture and a milder taste than older, drier ones.

Mayacoba

The mayacoba was developed in Mexico in the late 1970s when two other common beans were crossed in an effort to improve crop yield and quality. It was named after a Mexican village. This is a small bean, yellow in color, with a mild, buttery flavor. Many people believe it is more gentle on the digestive tract than other beans.

Mayacobas are used in casseroles and chilis, and as an alternative in any recipe that calls for pinto beans. The mayacoba is also known as the canary bean, due to its pale yellow shape and its little white eye.

Soup with mayacobas, celery, carrots, potatoes, tomatoes, leeks, and green onions.

Fast Fact

"Canary bean" is just one nickname for the mayacoba. It is also known as the Peruano, canario, maicoba, and Mexican yellow bean.

Navy Beans

These small, oval dry beans originated in South America thousands of years ago and are also known as white pea beans. In Spain they are called *alubias chica*. White in color with a slightly polished appearance, navy beans have a vaguely nautical appearance, but that is not the reason for their name. Rather, since the mid-1800s, they have been a staple food for the U.S. Navy, mainly because they are inexpensive and easy to store. They are also sometimes referred to as Yankee beans.

Their flavor is mild but hints of bacon. They pair well with savory spices, such as thyme and rosemary, and with various hearty flavors. They are one of the most commonly used beans and are often served in baked bean dishes, such as French cassoulet. They are also popular in soups.

Fast Fact

Some ancient people, including the followers of the Greek philosopher Pythagoras, thought human souls were transported to Hades via the stems and roots of bean plants. Eating legumes, or walking among them, was therefore forbidden. Another Greek philosopher, Aristotle, also considered legumes to be the gateway to Hades.

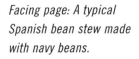

Facing page: A typical Spanish bean stew made with navy beans.

207

Fast Fact

Some people are sensitive to sulfites, a preservative added to many types of prepared foods. Unpleasant reactions include an increased heartbeat, disorientation, headaches, and other problems. Pinto beans are an excellent source of the mineral molybdenum, which helps to cleanse sulfites from the body.

Cooked pintos.

Pinto

The word *pinto* means "painted" in Spanish, and when these tan or cream dry beans are raw, they are covered in reddish-brown splotches. The pattern is lost when the beans are cooked, but it is replaced by a dusty, uniform pink. This bean is a cousin of navy and kidney beans, is thought to be native to Central and South America, and is especially popular in chilis. Pinto beans can be pureed and used in burritos and tacos, added whole to salads, or served on

A hearty stew made with pintos, meat, and vegetables.

their own, accompanied by seasonings and perhaps a small amount of butter or olive oil. Like other dry beans, they are a good source of limited protein, dietary fiber, vitamins, and minerals.

These beans spread to the United States and later to Europe, Africa, and Asia. They are one of the most commonly eaten beans in the United States.

Fast Fact

Because of the size and weight of its pods, the rattlesnake vine needs a strong support structure on which to grow. Some people who grow them pick a few pods when they reach about six inches in length, eat them fresh, and leave the rest on the vine to dry. The harvesters know the dry beans are ready when the vine's leaves turn brown and the pods acquire a papery texture.

Rattlesnake

As their name suggests, the pods of these fabulous beans are slender in shape and have snakelike markings. The dry beans within are speckled brown and auburn and are used, after soaking and cooking, in all kinds of soups, stews, and chili. The entire pod can also be eaten fresh, when it is steamed and lightly boiled. The young pod is green with purple streaks; it changes to shades of cream and brown when dried.

Rattlesnake pods on the vine.

Soldier

These long, white dry beans have distinctive red markings that give them a "toy soldier" appearance. They are ideal for baking and for adding to soups, and can be used in place of any other white bean in most recipes. They have a firm texture and mild flavor. Their markings tend to fade when cooked, but slow cooking can help prevent that.

Rattlesnake beans.

Soldier beans.

Swedish Brown

The Swedish brown, or *bruna bönor*, is a variety of dry bean that was developed in Sweden in the 1880s. These are small oval beans, pale to dark tan in color, with a small, distinctive white eye. They have a nutty, slightly sweet flavor. They hold their shape well when cooked, making them a popular addition to soups, stews, and casseroles—especially in Sweden, where they are used to make a traditional *bruna bönor* dish.

The traditional Swedish bruna bönor *dish made with Swedish brown beans.*

Fast Fact

Christopher Columbus introduced the beans of the Americas to Europe in the late fifteenth and early sixteenth centuries, and in 1533, Catherine de' Medici, the future wife of Henry II of France, carried a bag of beans (given to her as a wedding gift) when she arrived in Marseilles. But it was not until the seventeenth century that the bishop of Tarbes bestowed upon his countrymen a truly French flavor in the form of the Tarbais.

Tarbais

The Tarbais is the preferred dry bean for making the slow-cooked French casserole known as cassoulet. Although similar beans were introduced to Europe by Christopher Columbus, it was the bishop of Tarbes in southwestern France who, in the seventeenth century, established this bean as a part of French cuisine. He grew the bean in his garden and then introduced it to local farmers. It adapted well to the climate, and is today still considered by many in the region to be the only suitable bean for a cassoulet. A large white bean with a milky, tender flesh, the Tarbais mostly remains whole while cooking in a cassoulet, but some will burst and thicken the dish.

In France, the beans can be picked fresh, but most are left to dry on the vine. They were popular during the seventeenth and eighteenth centuries, but began to fall from favor in the mid-twentieth century. Efforts to protect the bean from dying out began in the mid-1980s, culminating in its attainment of PGI status (see page 241) in 2000. This means only

those beans grown and harvested by traditional methods in the Tarbais region can be labeled as "Tarbais," protecting both the heritage and qualities of the bean. Tarbais beans are all of one variety, Alaric. They are indeed the champagne of beans.

Tarbais beans are noted for their low starch content compared with other dry beans, and also for their thick skin that makes them easier to cook and contributes to their delicate flavor. They are said to melt in the mouth once cooked. In many ways, the Tarbais is such a prized bean that it seems its use should be reserved exclusively for cassoulet, but it can also be used in any recipe calling for white beans. These beans also work well in salads.

A traditional French cassoulet.

Tiger's Eye

Another common bean of Central and South American origin, the tiger's eye's main claim to fame, apart from its striking pattern, is its smooth texture and tender, fine skin that dissolves during cooking. The bean's pod, in contrast, is hard when mature, while the magnificent seeds within are amber in color with irregular slashes of maroon that are reminiscent of the flash of a tiger's eye. This is generally used as a dry bean, although people say that the young, immature beans, which are white in color and have faint pink specks or patterns, can be eaten fresh like snap peas.

A packet of tiger's eye seeds.

Tongue of Fire

The tongue of fire dry bean originated in the southernmost tip of South America in ancient times but has since become a favorite in Italy, where it is known as *Borlotto lingua di fuoca*. It is appreciated for its ability to adopt the flavors of other ingredients in cooking, but its dramatic appearance also carries great appeal. The pods are flat and pale green or white, lashed with a striking red pattern. The seeds inside are speckled in shades of red on a cream or white base.

The young, freshly picked beans are cooked and then eaten whole, whereas mature beans are shelled and the seeds dried for later use as dry beans. Tongues of fire have a creamy texture and a mild nutty flavor. They are used in all kinds of dishes, including casseroles, soups, stews, salads, and side dishes, although most of their markings will fade on cooking.

Tongue of fire pods on the vine.

Fast Fact

The United States grows the highest volume and greatest diversity of legumes in the world.

Tongue of fire beans and pods.

Yellow Eyes

Oval in shape and ivory in color, this common bean is also known as the dot-eye bean and molasses-face bean. Its hallmark feature is a large mustard-toned splotch, in the middle of which sits a white eye surrounded by a darker brown ring. They are about ½ inch in length. These dry beans have a mild, slightly sweet flavor and a mealy texture, and they hold their shape well when cooked. They are often paired with mushrooms, and work well in spicy African and Indian dishes, as well as in Italian-style soups.

Fast Fact

In 1907 Senator Knute Nelson from Minnesota introduced a resolution stating that bean soup must be served every day while the senate was in session.

Soup made with yellow eye beans.

Fast Fact

Fava Beans *(Vicia faba)*

This delicious legume is native to North Africa and parts of Asia but found its way to Mediterranean regions around 6000 BC. It became a favorite food of the ancient Romans and Greeks. Today, fava beans are widely cultivated and enjoyed in many countries and by many cultures.

The large, inedible pods look something like an oversized sweet pea, while the big, plump beans inside resemble smooth pebbles. Fava beans have a delightful subtle yet sweet flavor and creamy texture.

These legumes are often dried, but are also eaten fresh, either raw or cooked. They are best when young and tender.

Cooked favas served with herbs.

Preparation can be tedious, however. Not only do the beans need to be shelled from the pods, but the beans themselves are encased in a tough skin that also needs to be removed. The easiest way to do this is to blanch the shelled beans in boiling water for about thirty seconds and then pop them out of their skins. They can also be fried with the skin on, which will cause the skin to split. The skins are edible, but can be tough.

Fava beans lend themselves to many dishes that call for beans, from soups to dips; they are often an ingredient in vegetable stuffings, salads, and stews, and make great side dishes. They combine well with garlic and onions, and work well in broth-based risottos. Dried, fried, and salted fava beans make a delicious snack.

Fava pods on the plant.

Fast Fact

It is said that the beans Jack used in the fairy tale "Jack and the Beanstalk" were fava beans.

Toasted and salted fava beans.

Lentils *(Lens culinaris)*

This group of seeds encompasses a wide range of small dried legumes that are shaped like an optical lens, hence their name. They originated in the Middle East at least 10,000 years ago before spreading to Europe, Egypt, Asia, and eventually the Americas. Today, most are grown in India. They are one of the oldest crops to be domesticated.

The many varieties of lentils include shelled and not shelled, split and whole, and various colors, including yellow, orange, green, brown, and black. They are all small—some are very small, such as the green Estonia lentil. Like other legumes, lentils boast good quantities of plant protein, fiber, and various other nutrients, but they have the distinct advantage of being quick to cook. Most do not require soaking. A thorough washing, rinsing, and boiling for 15 to 30 minutes will do. Their mild, earthy flavor works best when combined with more potent flavors such as garlic, turmeric, ginger, and curry. A few of the most popular types are discussed in this section.

Split lentils are called dal in India and are one of the key ingredients in the spicy Indian dish of the same name.

Above: Assorted lentils.
Facing page: Lentil curry.

Fast Fact

Lentils are the richest source of folate among plant foods.

From top: Brown lentils, red lentils, pink lentils.
Right: Chana del lentils.

Brown

Brown lentils are widely available and often purchased dried or in cans. They have an earthy flavor and can become mushy if cooked for too long.

Chana Dal

This small lentil looks like a split pea. When cooked, it swells to about the size of a corn kernel. It has a rich, earthy flavor and is an important ingredient in dal. Chana dal are easily digested and full of nutrients such as folic acid, potassium, phosphorus, magnesium, and zinc. Like other legumes, they are also a great source of plant protein, dietary fiber, and low-GI carbs.

Chana dals blend well with spices such as garlic, cardamom, and cloves. Unlike most lentils, they are generally soaked for at least a few hours, and then will cook in about 10 minutes. They add taste and texture to various curries, fritters, casseroles, and

salads. Roasted chana dal are also powdered into a flour that is widely used in Indian cuisine.

Puy

Also known as French green lentils, this variety was originally grown in the volcanic soils of Puy, France. Puy lentils have a light

Puy lentils.

peppery flavor, hold their shape well upon cooking, and are considered the best of the lentils. They do, however, take longer to cook (about 40 minutes) than other varieties.

Red

Red lentils are especially quick to cook, but fade in color and lose their shape. They have a mild, slightly sweet flavor and work well in dals where loss of shape is of no concern.

Other Varieties

Other types include:

- pink lentils, known as masoor dal, which is a split masoor lentil.
- beluga lentils, a small black lentil that glistens when cooked and is thought to resemble beluga caviar.
- masoor lentils, which are greenish-brown in color.
- toor dal, which is a dried and split pigeon pea (see page 234).
- chana dal and Bengal gram, varieties of peeled and split chickpeas (see page 181).
- urad dal, in fact a urad bean (see page 253).
- moong dal lentils, which are skinned and split mung beans (see page 248).

From top: Beluga lentils; dal made with chana dal lentils.

Cooking with Lentils

Lentils of all kinds are the main ingredient of Indian-style dals, but they are also popular in curries, soups, and casseroles, or as a side dish cooked with garlic, onions, and other ingredients. Lentils can also be ground into a flour that is used to make pakora batter or as a thickener in curries. They are also used to make papadums, the crisp, fried wafers that are eaten with Indian curries.

Lentil sprouts are highly nutritious and are used as a crunchy addition to salads, stir-fries, casseroles, and stews. It is thought that because they are a sprouted legume they have higher levels of nutrients. The sprouts are low in calories but high in B vitamins (including folate), the antioxidant vitamin C, and potassium. Like all legumes, they are a good source of plant protein, but they lack the amino acid methionone.

Pakoras in lentil batter.

Lima Beans
(*Phaseolus lunatus*)

Limas come from Central and South America and are named for the capital city of Peru. Although they are nutritionally similar to common beans, they belong to a different category, and overall tend to have slightly lower amounts of protein and considerably less folate. Their botanical name, *Phaseolus lunatus*, meaning "half-moon-shaped bean," is a reference to their crescent shape. Two of the most popular types of limas are the Christmas lima and the butter bean.

Lima bean pods.

Butter Bean

Butter beans, also known simply as lima beans, are thought to have originated in parts of South and Central America, and were first cultivated in Peru over 7,000 years ago. They were a staple food and vital source of protein for the Mayans, Aztecs, and Incas. There are many different types, but they fall into two main categories: the bush variety that, as the name suggests, grow on a bush, and the vine or pole variety that thrive on a trellis.

Soup made with lima beans.

Bush butter beans are the smaller of the two types. Both the larger and smaller beans are kidney-shaped and green or white. Both types should be soaked and boiled before eating, due to the presence of cyanide compounds in the raw beans. They are not suitable for grinding into flour.

Although high in a range of health-promoting nutrients, butter beans are especially high in the trace mineral molybdenum, which helps to detoxify sulfites in the beans.

All butter beans share a buttery texture and a sweet flavor. Smaller butter beans are less likely to become mushy on cooking than larger ones, but they all work well in a variety of dishes including salads, soups, and casseroles. They are also great for making healthy homemade versions of refried beans, as a filling for tacos, or as a tasty side dish in place of mashed potatoes.

Fast Facts

Butter beans are usually purchased as dry beans, but freshly shelled seeds that have not been dried are also very tasty and nutritious.

Fast Fact

Lima beans were first cultivated in Peru and are named for its capital city, Lima. Cultivation in many countries, including the United States, is restricted to certain varieties that have low toxicity. Other varieties can be highly toxic if not prepared and cooked thoroughly.

Christmas Lima

Christmas lima beans hail from the Peruvian Andes, where they have been grown since at least 1500 BC. They are heirloom beans that gained popularity in South America during the 1800s before being replaced by commercially grown bean varieties in the twentieth century. Today, they are making a comeback as a favored heirloom variety. Their various other names include chestnut lima, speckled lima, and (somewhat confusingly) butter bean. They are large and

Christmas lima bean stew.

cream-colored with maroon markings that remain after cooking. Their texture is creamy and their flavor nutty, a little like chestnut. This flavor combined with their festive markings are responsible for the "Christmas" descriptor.

Christmas limas are a wholesome addition to winter soups and stews. They also make a delicious side dish if warmed with some herbs and drizzled with a little olive oil.

Raw Christmas lima beans.

Fast Fact

Lupini beans were a favorite of the ancient Romans and remain popular in Italy today. Processing them is labor-intensive, however, and carries some risk due to toxic compounds in the raw beans. But fortunately, pickled lupinis are also available and ready to eat.

Lupini Beans

(*Lupinus albus*)

This bean has two distinct qualities: it contains all the essential amino acids, and it is potentially toxic, which seems to have limited its popularity over time. There are many varieties of this legume, which has its origins in the Mediterranean region. The popular variety found in Italy is the white lupini bean.

Lupinis were originally grown as ornamental plants before the ancient Romans recognized them as a valuable food source. They are naturally high in poison-ous, bitter alkaloids that must be drawn out to make the beans edible. This is done by soaking them in brine for several days. Recently, some less bitter, low-alkaloid variet-ies have been developed, but even those must be prepared properly before eating. Lupinis are generally sold dry or pickled in brine, but even with these precautions, some people remain sensitive to the alkaloids.

Lupini served with beer.

When properly prepared, the bitter flavor of the lupinis subsides and a nutty flavor remains. They are large, flat, and yellowish-cream in color. Lupinis have thick, tough skins, and part of the fun of eating them is using your teeth to bite into the tough outer skin and pop out the bean within. The skin is then discarded. In this form, lupinis are often served in Italy as a savory snack with beer and other refreshments.

Lupini flowers.

In terms of nutrition, lupini beans contain almost as much protein as soybeans but have about one-third fewer calories. Although they are usually eaten as a snack, some of the newer varieties are ground into high-protein flours or used to make tofu.

Fast Fact

Beans were so revered by the ancient Romans that four great families named themselves accordingly: They were the Lentullus family (named for the lentil), the Piso family (named for peas), the Cicero family (named for the chickpea), and the Fabius family (named for the fava bean).

Facing page: Yellow pea soup.

Below: Boiled split green peas.

Peas (*Pisum sativum*)

Green peas, yellow peas, split peas, snow peas, and snap peas—all are varieties of the same plant, and they are legumes. Native to the Middle East and parts of Asia, these peas date back 10,000 years or more. They were one of the first crops cultivated by humans, although in ancient times they were eaten dried, rather than fresh. Today, they are grown all around the world. Some are picked and eaten young, pod and bean together (see page 260). Others are harvested when the pod is mature, and the seeds are then dried and the skins removed, after which they split naturally. Peas should be soaked for several hours overnight before boiling, and then they can be used in soups and stews.

Peas are compact in size, high in fiber, and full of various antioxidants such as vitamins C and E. They are also higher in starch and lower in protein than most other legumes, although the fresh varieties have less starch than dried or cooked ones. The small amount of fat peas contain is of the healthy omega-3 type. They also contain a phytonutrient called coumestrol that is being researched for possibly offering protection against stomach cancer.

Fast Fact

Pigeon pea plants have many uses: Their low, shrubby bushes can form hedges that act as windbreaks, and their stems are used to make thatched roofs and fences.

Pigeon pea pods.

Pigeon Peas *(Cajunus cajun)*

The term "pigeon pea" is often used to describe various dried peas and lentils, but actually refers to a specific species, *Cajanus cajan*, sometimes called the "Congo pea." Although their geographic origins are uncertain, pigeon peas were first cultivated in India and Egypt at least 3,500 years ago, before spreading to Asia, Africa, Europe, and the Americas.

The pigeon pea is a drought-resistant legume that now grows in many warm, dry regions. The green pod is small, less than three inches long, and houses between two and nine seeds that are generally green or yellow, but can also be brown, purple, white, black, or variegated. The young green seeds and sometimes the pods are eaten freshly cooked as a vegetable, whereas mature seeds are dried, split, and then used to make dal or added to soups, stews, and chilis. In India, the dried pigeon pea is known as toor dal, and it can also be ground into flour.

Pigeon peas are a good source of limited plant protein. The mature seed is comprised of about 20 percent protein, along with other nutrients, including carbs, fiber, and various vitamins and minerals. The young pea contains less protein (less than 10 percent). Pigeon peas are also used as feed for livestock.

Toor dal.

Runners *(Phaseolus coccineus)*

The varieties of this dry bean include scarlet runners, white runners, and also the larger gigantes and elephantes that are especially popular in Greece. All have similar nutritional qualities: they are particularly high in protein (about 20 percent of the total composition) and low-GI carbs (about 43 percent), they have almost no fat, and they are rich sources of dietary fiber. They also provide good amounts of calcium, potassium, phosphorus, vitamin C, and B vitamins, among other nutrients. The main differences between the various types is in their size and the color of their seeds.

The seeds come in a wide range of colors, including white, scarlet, and black, and they match the color of the flowers on the corresponding plant. The color of the seeds indicates the different types of antioxidant plant pigments found in them. So, despite their nutritional similarities, there are differences on a micronutritional level. The term "runner" refers to the plant's habit of running up poles, trees, and fences.

Fast Fact

Runners grown on a trellis are well suited to drying. Their height means the pods hang high, where they are less likely to rot. The big pods also mean more seeds per pod, so less shelling is needed to gather a good number of seeds.

Facing page: The white runner's white flowers.

Below: White beans from the same plant.

Fast Fact

In Greece, gigantes and elephantes are commonly included in *mezze*, a selection of small, tasty dishes that are usually served as appetizers.

Facing page: A Greek delicacy, the enormous white gigantes bean.

Thought to be native to Central America, runners were probably first domesticated about 2,000 years ago. In ancient times, they were eaten both fresh and dried, and valued for their nutritious tuberous roots. Finding their way to Europe in the 1500s, they were first grown as an ornamental plant because of their colorful, showy flowers before being adopted as a food. Today, the dried beans are used in soups, and stews, or as a side dish cooked with onions, tomatoes, and spices. Young pods that have not been dried are also eaten as fresh vegetables (see page 262).

Elephantes and Gigantes

The gigantes is a large and plump cousin of the white and scarlet runners, while the elephantes is an even bigger, fatter cousin. The elephantes are 20 to 30 percent heavier than the gigantes. As their names suggest, the primary difference between these beans and the smaller scarlet and white runners is also in their size, especially after soaking.

The gigantes and the elephantes are both grown in sheltered plateaus in the Kastoria region of Greece, where abundant water, humidity, and fertile soils are all ideal for growing these oversized beans.

Both varieties are afforded Protected Geographical Indication (PGI) accreditation, which means they can be grown only in specified regions of Greece, in much the same way that the appellation system operates in France to protect French wines and other produce.

Both gigantes and elephantes are enormously popular in Greece, often served marinated in olive oil and spices in a similar way to Italian olives, or used to make garlic dips such as *skordalia*. Because elephantes can be difficult to find, lima or kidney beans are used more often but inevitably lack some of the impressive power, punch, and robust presence of this oversized variety.

Facing page: Elephantes served with salad.
Below: Baked gigantes.

Fast Fact

Protected Geographical Indication (PGI) accreditation is common in Europe, and it means that the geographic region where a specific type of produce is grown defines the produce. If a bean with PGI accreditation is grown outside its assigned location, for example, it cannot have the same name and is considered a different type of bean. This system allows the regions of Europe to maintain their hold on specific produce and protects the produce's cultural significance. The European Union established the terms for this system in 1992, and certain beans, including the gigantes of Greece, have PGI status.

Fast Fact

Scarlet runners are just one type of bean used to make *ama-natto*, the Japanese dish of sweetened whole beans—adzuki beans are also commonly used. Another Japanese speciality, *natto*, is made from fermented soybeans and is not sweet in flavor. It is an acquired taste, and the fermented beans have a pungent smell that is sometimes compared to cheese. *Natto* is often eaten with mustard or soy sauce.

Scarlet Runners

The scarlet seeds of this bean, once dried, are used in soups and stews, served warm as a side dish, or pureed together with other ingredients such as tahini to make delicious, nutritious dips. Like most other beans, they must be soaked and boiled before eating. They are large in size, and have a smooth, creamy texture and a mild, buttery flavor. Scarlet runner beans are put to a special use in Japan; the mature dried beans are boiled and sweetened with sugar or molasses to make an unusual sweet dish known as *ama-natto*.

White Runners

Also known as the white emergo, white runner beans are similar to other types of runners in terms of physical characteristics, flavor, and nutritional benefits, but the color of their seeds and flowers is white. Like scarlet runners, they are enjoyed as a side dish or can be added to soups, stews, and various tasty and nutritious dips.

Facing page: The deep pink flowers of the scarlet runner.

Other Dry Beans

A few more popular varieties of dry beans are discussed below.

Adzuki (*Vigna angularis*)

This sweet, nutty bean is popular in Japan, where it is cooked, pureed, and sweetened to make a paste called *anko* that is used in desserts. It is equally at home in savory dishes such as soup and stews, and can also be ground into flour and used in baking. Small in size and red-brown in color, it has a distinctive cream seam. It is thought to have originated in China before spreading to Japan and then Africa, Asia, and the Americas.

Adzukis boast a high number of micronutrients and are rich in folate and manganese. Low in fat, they are also a good source of soluble fiber, low-GI carbohydrates, and protein (although they lack the amino acid methionine). To prepare adzuki beans, soak them overnight and simmer in water for about an hour. Because soaking causes the beans' color to fade and weakens their shape, they can also be simmered for a longer period without prior soaking.

Fast Fact

The word *adzuki* means "little bean" in Japanese. The color red is often featured in Asian celebrations and feasts, and so this legume is also celebrated on account of its rich red color.

Facing page: Adzuki pods.

Below: Adzuki beans.

Fast Fact

The little black eye in the center of the black-eyed pea was once called *mogette*, meaning "nun" in French, because it was thought to resemble a nun's habit.

Black-Eyed Pea

(*Vigna unguiculata*)

This little bean is creamy-white in color with a black "eye" mark at its sprouting point. It is one of the few beans that requires only a short soaking time before cooking. Like all legumes, the black-eyed pea is a good source of protein, low-GI carbohydrates, fiber, and various vitamins and minerals. Of special note is that black-eyed peas are high in vitamin K, with half a cup providing about a quarter of the daily recommended intake.

In the American South, black-eyed peas are traditionally served on New Year's Day to bring good luck for the new year. They have a mild savory flavor and make a lovely side dish when cooked with spices and broths. They are also delicious in stews, casseroles, and soups.

Cooked black-eyed peas in a salad.

Moth Bean (*Vigna aconitifolia*)

This tiny bean is about the size and shape of a medium or long grain of rice. It is the seed of the South Asian matki plant and is highly valued for its ability to survive in drought-stricken climates. Like most other legumes, its nitrogen-fixing ability is also of special importance.

This legume is sometimes called matki or Turkish gram, and it ranges in color from tan to dark brown. The pulses should be soaked overnight and boiled before being used in dals, curries, soups, and other Indian dishes. Beans left to soak for longer will sprout and should also develop a slightly sweeter flavor. They can then be used in salads and dishes such as misal, a spiced breakfast dish of the western Indian state of Maharashtra.

Moth beans can also be roasted and ground to produce a coarse flour that can be used as a thickening agent or in various baked goods.

Fast Fact

Moth beans grow in some of the world's most inhospitable climates. They can survive droughts, drying winds, and other challenges. Abundant moth bean crops are grown in semiarid regions of northwestern India.

Fast Fact

Just one pound of mung bean seeds can produce about six pounds of bean sprouts.

Mung Beans (*Vigna radiata*)

These beans have been used in Asian cuisine for thousands of years and are now cultivated in India, China, parts of Europe, and parts of the United States. Mung beans are small and green in color, but once their outer skin is removed, their mustard-yellow interior is revealed. Mung beans are prized for their antioxidant and detoxifying properties, and are noted for their phytoestrogens, which mimic the hormone estrogen and may help relieve symptoms of menopause.

In cooking, mung beans work well in both savory and sweet recipes. Usually purchased in dried form, they must be soaked before being added to soups,

An Indonesian mung bean dessert with coconut milk and palm sugar.

casseroles, stir-fries, and other dishes. They are quick to cook and will be ready in less than a minute when stir-fried. They are also used to make noodles and flour and are said to be more gentle on the digestive tract than most other legumes.

Vegetable soup with mung beans.

Sprouted mung beans are known as bean sprouts. They are the large, whitish-gray sprouts with yellow tips that are widely used in stir-fries and salads. Mung bean paste is produced by soaking, cooking, and pureeing the beans into a paste that is used in various desserts, including ice cream. Moong dal lentils are mung beans that have had their skins removed and have been dried, after which they split naturally (see page 223).

Bean sprouts and mung beans.

Fast Fact

In Japan, the rice bean is known as *tsura-adzuki* because of its similarity to the adzuki. It is sometimes sold as a substitute for the adzuki.

Rice Beans (*Vigna umbellata*)

The rice bean probably originated in China, and today it is grown mainly in China, India, Bangladesh, and Nepal. Although the young pods are sometimes eaten fresh, the beans are more often dried, and then soaked before cooking. They can also be sprouted. Although lower in protein than most other legumes, it is a nutritious food that is used in dals and sauces.

The rice bean is considered a relatively minor food source, but may potentially become more important, not least because of its ability to grow in hilly terrain. It is valuable as green manure. The name "rice bean" may refer to the fact that it is often grown after rice harvesting as an intercrop to restore the nitrogen in the soil, rather than because the bean has any particular ricelike characteristics.

Tepary (*Phaseolus acutifolius*)

A native of Central America, this bean was first cultivated at least 5,000 years ago and was later introduced to parts of Africa where it is well suited to hot, dry conditions. The small, green pod is covered in a fine fuzz, and the seeds inside range in color from greenish-yellow to purplish-brown and red. After shelling, the seeds are dried and must be soaked and cooked before eating. Tepary beans are widely used in stir-fries and similar dishes throughout Asia.

Fast Fact

The tepary is considered to be one of the most drought-tolerant legumes in the world—not surprising, really, given that it is a native of the Sonoran Desert in southwestern North America. It is so drought-resistant that too much moisture can have a detrimental effect, nutritionally, because it leads to a surplus of foliage and a lower yield of legumes.

Toloso (*Phaseolus volubilis*)

The town of Tolosa, Spain, values its beans so highly that it holds a festival in their honor every November, when the cooked beans are distributed throughout town. This prized bean, a regional specialty, is egg-shaped and glossy black, but fades to purple when cooked. It has a buttery flavor. It is rarely cooked with anything but the water in which it was boiled and perhaps a splash of oil and herbs.

In 1999 Toloso beans were granted the Kalitatea mark (Basque Food Quality Label) in recognition of their quality. The mark confirms that the beans have been grown according to ancestral techniques and with respect for the natural environment.

Toloso, Spain.

Urad Beans (*Vigna mungo*)

The urad bean is also known as the black gram or urad dal bean. It is a whole dried bean and is black in color. The flesh inside the urad bean is white, however, and when the skin has been removed, it is commonly called a white lentil. Urad beans are soaked, boiled, and eaten whole, or used to make dal.

Fast Fact

The urad bean is highly valued in India and is particularly beneficial for women's health due to its rich supply of iron, folic acid, and calcium.

Fresh Peas and Beans

Fresh beans and shelled peas (which are undried seeds) do not require soaking and are eaten raw or cooked as fresh vegetables, with or without the pod. These include French beans, garden peas, wax beans, and snow peas. They are much lighter and less "meaty" than dry beans and, because they have not been dehydrated, they also have a much higher water content. When eaten raw, crisp bean pods have a fresh, slightly sweet flavor, while fresh peas have a sweet and slightly nutty taste and a firm texture. Steaming or boiling will soften the textures and dull the subtle flavors, but the cooked vegetables pair well with other ingredients such as onions, garlic, and herbs, either served warm or in salads.

Fresh peas and beans differ greatly from dry beans, not just in taste, texture, and appearance but also in

terms of nutrition—even when both come from the same plant. For example, dry split peas and fresh green peas are both from the same plant (*Pisum sativum*), but they have vastly different nutritional profiles.

Generally, on account of their high water content, fresh beans provide only about a third of the fiber offered by dry beans and comparatively low amounts of protein and carbohydrates. Nonetheless, they contain many vitamins, minerals, and phytonutrients and are also low in calories, so they make a nutritious addition to any meal. In comparison, fresh green peas have relatively high amounts of protein, carbohydrates, and fiber (see page 260).

It should be noted that some authors categorize fresh beans and green peas differently from other beans for nutritional reasons, and do not include them in discussions of legumes. Both are, however, classified botanically as members of the bean family, and so are discussed here.

Green beans with their tops and tails intact.

Fast Fact

Fresh green beans were once commonly known as string beans, but when botanists learned how to cultivate a stringless variety in the late 1800s, the stringed ones (and their name) became less common.

Green Beans

(Phaseolus vulgaris)

Fresh green beans are also known as string beans, snap beans, and haricots vert (French for "green beans"). They are not dried but are eaten whole, pod and seed. Usually they are cooked and served hot, but they are also added cold to salads and may be served raw. Fresh, young, raw beans are crisp and sweet; the best ones snap open easily to reveal a moist, gelatinous substance surrounding the beans inside.

Cooked green beans are best if steamed for five minutes so they retain some of their crispness, although some recipes call for softer beans that have been cooked longer. Green beans are also readily available frozen or canned, but fresh beans retain the most nutrients.

Green beans contain some protein, but not as much as in other legumes. Most of their calories are derived from carbohydrates. They are a good source of dietary fiber and certain vitamins and minerals, including folate, magnesium, and vitamins A and C. Green beans are also a good source of other antioxidants, including carotenoids (such as beta-carotene and lutein) that are more commonly associated with orange or red vegetables. The chlorophyll pigments in green beans mask the color of those carotenoids.

Green beans grown in the United States account for approximately 60 percent of the world's production, but they are also widely grown and popular in France, Italy, Iraq, and Argentina. In Italy, for example, they are mixed with gnocchi and pesto to make a delicious dish called gnocchi alla Genovese.

Some green beans still have strings, a fibrous seam that runs along both sides of the pod. This is generally removed before cooking. Stringless varieties were first cultivated in the late 1800s and, when available, are often preferred because they are easier to prepare.

Fast Fact

Fresh green beans are high in water and low in calories, containing only about 30 calories per 3½ ounces.

Green bean salad.

Fast Fact

Although all legumes provide folate, fresh long beans are one of the best sources. Folate is especially important for expectant mothers, and has a role in preventing neural tube defects in babies.

Long Beans

(*Vigna unguiculata*)

Also known as the yard-long bean, this legume, as its name suggests, has an exceptionally long pod—not quite a yard in length, but usually at least half that. Long beans grow in the tropical regions of Asia and are eaten whole, as a side dish, or in stir-fries, rice, and noodle dishes. The long, intertwining pods add a fascinating visual touch to any dish, although the beans are usually sliced diagonally into smaller, thinner pieces to make them easier to eat. This bean also looks spectacular when growing on its plant.

There are several varieties of this bean that bear mature seeds in a range of different colors.

Peas *(Pisum sativum)*

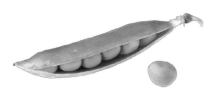

From top: Snap pea, sugar pea, garden peas.

Although fresh green peas can be eaten raw, they are generally preferred boiled or steamed and served with meat dishes. One popular Italian side dish mixes peas in a sauce of sautéed onions, tomatoes, seasonings, and sometimes ham.

Fresh green peas are a good plant source of protein, offering about half the amount of protein per serving than that provided by most dry beans. They are also a good source of carbohydrates and dietary fiber, as well as various vitamins, minerals, and phytonutrients. They are especially rich in vitamin C.

Snow peas and snap peas are popular types of fresh peas. Their pods, including the seeds, are often eaten. They are

Peas in the pod.

generally lightly steamed and then mixed into salads or stir-fries. These two types are similar in appearance, but the snow pea pod is longer and thinner than the fleshy, crisp snap pea.

Peas can also be dried, and dried peas tend to be more nutritious than snap peas and snow peas. Dried peas are also higher in starch.

Fast Fact

In Great Britain, etiquette dictates that the correct way to eat peas is to squish them onto the back of a fork, not to scoop them up with a fork or spoon.

Stir-fried snap peas, carrots, and baby corns.

Runner Beans

(*Phaseolus coccineus*)

This legume can be eaten as dried seeds (see page 237) or freshly picked, pod and all. Fresh runner beans are similar in appearance to green beans (see page 256) and are often confused with them— runner beans are longer and more slender. The runner also tends to be flatter and less fleshy than the green bean, causing the seeds inside the pod to press into the pod to give it a lumpier, slightly wavy profile. Confusingly, the names "runner" and "green bean" are often used interchangeably, and their common names can vary among different countries and regions.

The runner pods are best when young, as they become tougher and thicker as they mature. Runners have a stronger flavor and coarser flesh than the green bean, and are a stringed bean that ideally should be topped,

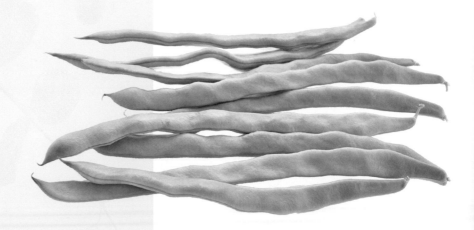

tailed, and destringed before cooking. They are usually sliced into elongated strips before cooking, and then included in stir-fries and similar dishes, or served as a simple side dish. The beans can also be left to mature on the vine, after which they are sometimes shelled and dried and used in a similar way to lima beans (see page 225).

Cooked and sliced runner beans.

Fast Fact

These low-fat, low-sodium, cholesterol-free legumes are also low in calories: half a cup of cooked wax beans contains only around 20 calories.

Facing page: Adding ingredients to a stir-fry of wax beans and other vegetables.

Wax Beans

(*Phaseolus vulgaris*)

The wax bean is closely related and looks similar to the green bean, except wax beans are a buttery yellow in color. They can be used with or in place of green beans in any number of recipes. Confusingly, they are sometimes referred to as butter beans (a term also used for baby lima beans). Like green beans, wax beans are picked and eaten fresh in their entirety, pod and seed, rather than dried, and their flavor is sweet and mild. Although these beans are now grown and eaten around the world, they come from North America, where Native Americans developed a specialized farming practice that included growing what they called the "three sisters"—beans, corn, and squash—together. This method enabled complementary use of the soil nutrients among the three crops and encouraged healthy plants.

Purple wax beans are also sometimes available, but turn green when cooked.

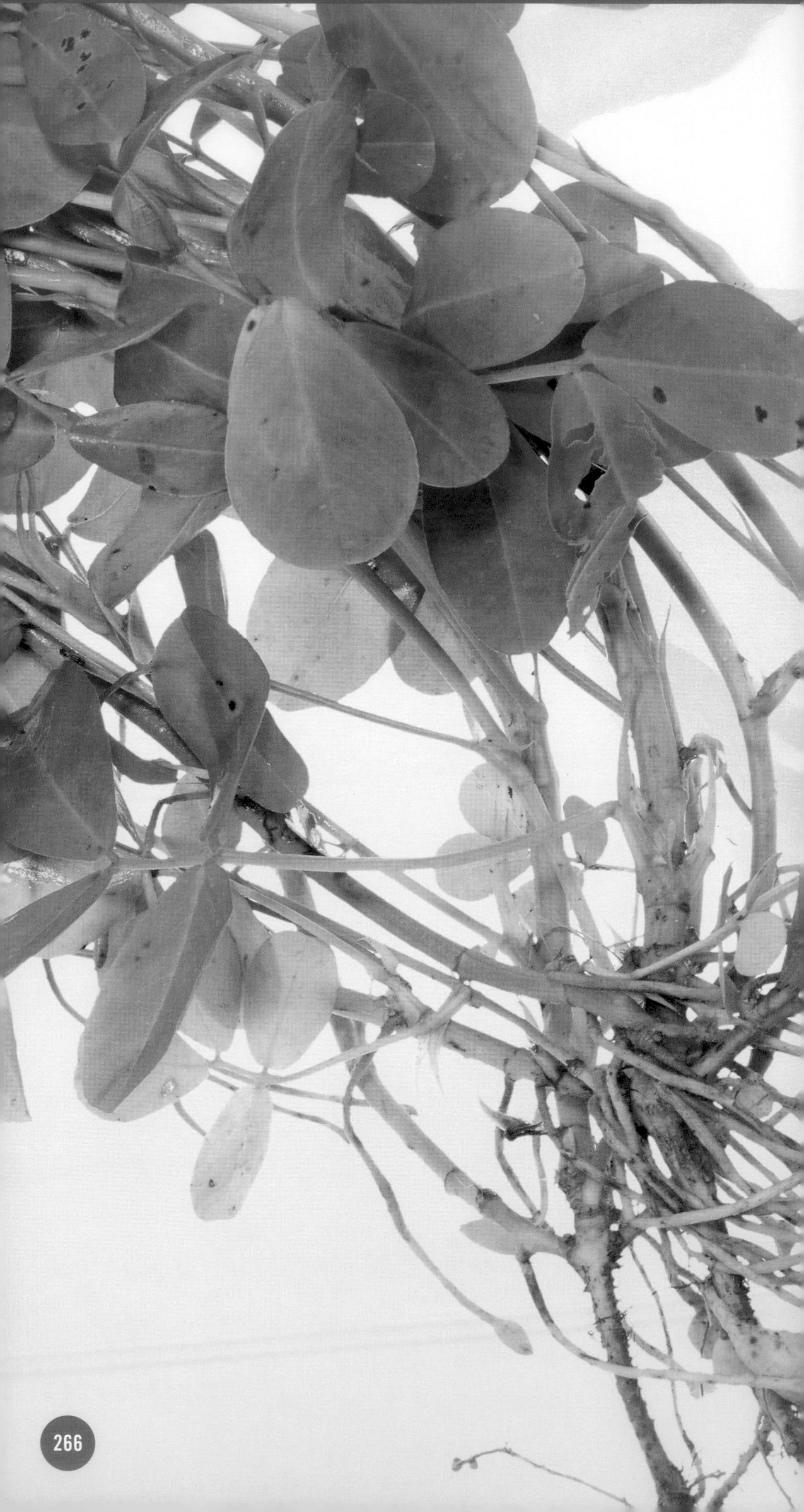

The Exceptions

Not all beans are created equal. Unlike most legumes, for example, soybeans and peanuts are both high in fat, in addition to being high in protein and other nutrients. Soybeans provide an added benefit in that they are a complete protein source. There are other legumes, such as alfalfa and mesquite, that are less commonly recognized as such. A selection of these exceptions are discussed on the following pages.

Alfalfa (*Medicago sativa*)

The alfalfa plant is commonly used as a forage crop for feeding livestock and as green manure because of its nitrogen-fixing abilities (see page 171). It belongs to the clover family. Native to Iran, it spread into Europe and China between 500 and 200 BC, and then elsewhere around the world. Although it grows best in temperate regions, its long roots enable it to survive in drier climates as well.

As a food, sprouted alfalfa is often added to salads to give extra crunch and flavor, or used on sandwiches in place of or together with lettuce. The sprouts are fine, and their flavor is subtle yet grassy. The white, loosely intertwined translucent sprouts topped with delicate green leaves have a fresh appearance that gives life to salads and also makes them an attractive garnish.

Nutritionally, alfalfa sprouts do offer some dietary fiber and protein, but their main benefits lie in their vitamins, minerals, and antioxidants. Alfalfa sprouts are a concentrated source of

Below: Alfalfa seeds; sprouting alfalfa.

vitamin K, the antioxidant beta-carotene, and other nutrients. They are also low in calories (only about 10 calories per cup).

Like all raw legume sprouts, however, alfalfa sprouts contain some toxins, so they should be eaten raw only in moderation, or should be cooked before eating.

In folk medicine, alfalfa has long been used to ease various digestive ailments such as ulcers, and to treat arthritis. Because the sprouts also have diuretic properties, they can help relieve fluid retention and assist in the treatment of urinary tract infections.

A fresh salad made with alfalfa sprouts and shaved cucumbers.

Let's Sprout!

Alfalfa sprouts are readily available from supermarkets, but can also be sprouted at home. One tablespoon of seeds should yield about 1½ cups of sprouts.

- First, rinse the seeds. Then place them in a clean jar and cover them in two inches of warm water.
- Cover the jar with cheesecloth or a similar material, secured by string or elastic. This will keep insects from getting in and will make it easier to drain the seeds in the coming days, because only the water will pass through the cheesecloth, leaving the seeds behind.
- Allow the seeds to soak overnight.
- The next day, drain them, rinse them, and then place them back in the jar in a single layer, not too close together. They should be moist but not drenched or submerged in water.
- Place the jar in a warm, dark place on its side (the sprouts don't need sunlight at this point).
- Thoroughly rinse and drain the seeds every morning and night as the seeds begin to sprout, remembering to place the jar on its side after rinsing. Once the sprouts are about two inches long, move the jar to a sunny spot.
- When the leaves turn green, they are ready to eat. The entire process should take only a few days.
- Once fully sprouted, the sprouts can be stored in the fridge, where they will continue to grow for a few more days as long as they do not dry out.

Fast Fact

Although they are called "beans," coffee beans and cocoa beans are not from the same family as bean (or legume) plants.

Carob (*Ceratonia siliqua*)

Although perhaps best known for providing an alternative to cocoa and chocolate, carob has a long history dating back to at least ancient Greek, Roman, and Egyptian times. The Romans are said to have enjoyed the sweet flavor of fresh young pods, while the Greeks likened it to a type of fig. The ancient Egyptians made use of the seed's gummy properties when binding their mummies.

Carob beans are native to the Mediterranean region, where they are eaten both fresh and dried. Fresh young beans are also edible, as are the pods, which can be used to make many things, including both carob powder and stock feed. In the United States, carob is most often eaten in its dried form as an alternative to chocolate and cocoa. Dried carob beans are ground to produce a powder that can flavor, thicken, or darken other foods. Carob is also used to produce a gelling agent known as locust bean gum, which is used in ice cream and other processed foods.

The carob pods have a curious appearance: long, curved, flat shapes punctuated by oval mounds formed by the seeds pushing out. The pods are green when young, but darken on the tree as they mature. They grow to be between 4 and 10 inches long. Nutritionally, carob is a particularly good source of calcium and certain antioxidants, including tannins.

Although they look a lot like carob seeds, cocoa beans, coffee beans, and vanilla beans are not legumes.

A hot carob drink made with carob powder and milk.

A Turkish sweet dessert with carob and molasses.

Fast Fact

Many people describe jicama as having the texture of a turnip but the flavor of an apple. Its thicker outer skin, vines, and leaves are toxic, however.

Jicama (*Pachyrhizus erosus*)

Also know as the yam bean, jicama is indeed a legume, with seed-bearing pods that grow on vines. In this case, however, it is the root of the jicama that is eaten, rather than its toxic seeds and pod. Therefore, it is generally thought of as a tuber vegetable. Jicama root is popular in many parts of Central America, Asia, and South America. It must be peeled, as its thick outer skin is inedible and contains a toxin called rotenone. Its white flesh is crisp and slightly sweet. Jicama is an excellent source of dietary fiber and antioxidants, including vitamin C.

Mesquite (*Prosopis* ssp.)

This legume is the long, creamy-beige pod of the mesquite tree, a common desert plant. Historically, the sweet and juicy seed inside the pod was a food staple, and an important source of protein for Native American tribes of the Southwest.

The pod and seed were hand-ground on rocks to produce a meal or flour that was then used to make simple, sun baked cakes and cookies.

Contemporary milling methods enable the mesquite pod and seed to be ground quickly into a nutritious, high fiber flour. Some claim that the pods can be boiled and eaten, or used in tealike infusions, but they are usually used as a thickener in soups, stews, and casseroles, or as a flour in baked goods. The seeds and pods are high in protein.

Fast Fact

Mesquite trees require a lot of water, leaving grasslands depleted of moisture and causing groundwater levels to drop.

From top: Mesquite pods growing on the tree; dried mesquite pods; mesquite flour.

Fast Fact

It is said to take close to 550 peanuts to make a 12-ounce jar of peanut butter.

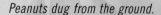

Peanuts dug from the ground.

Peanuts *(Arachis hypogaea)*

More often thought of as a nut, the peanut is actually a legume, and perhaps if it had been called a "nutbean," there would have been less confusion. Peanuts do have some nutlike features, including an edible seed housed inside a tough external shell. But that shell is actually a type of pod. And unlike nuts, peanuts grow underground and not on trees. They develop in an unusual way: Starting first as a flower, peanuts are pollinated and then lowered to the ground on a growing, lengthening stalk that then pushes it underground. Once underground, the flower's ovary develops into the pod, or shell, of the peanut.

The peanut has its origins in the Mesoamerican region, in what is now Central America. In ancient times, peanuts were an important food for the Aztecs, and today they grow in warm climates all around the world, especially Africa, Asia, and the United States. They became extremely popular in the United States during the nineteenth century, due largely to the fact that botanist George Washington Carver suggested that peanuts could become a hardy food source for poor sharecroppers and could provide them with an alternative cash crop to cotton, which suffered infestations by pests during the early 1900s.

The peanut is usually regarded and consumed as if it were a nut, eaten by the handful (or two) as a snack, or sprinkled over other foods to add a buttery crunch. Peanuts are also mixed into a wide range of savory dishes, including rice pilafs and salads, or crushed and pureed into peanut butter. They are also the main ingredient in the sweet and spicy satay sauce, widely used in Asian dishes such as *gado gado* or served with grilled chicken skewers. Their flavor and texture also blend well with toffee, honey, jams, and in sweets such as fudge.

Unlike most other legumes, the peanut is high in fat (mainly monounsaturated),

Fast Fact

George Washington Carver (c. 1864–1943) was born a slave in Missouri, but grew up to become a botanist, inventor, and teacher. Carver was especially interested in peanuts and found more than 100 uses for them, including in paints, plastics, dyes, and gasoline.

Peanuts growing in a field.

Fast Fact

The nutrients in peanuts may help to protect against cardiovascular disease. Not only do peanuts contain the antioxidant resveratrol, they also have copper, phosphorus, magnesium, iron, potassium, selenium, zinc, and calcium.

making it suitable for cooking oil. It is also a good source of antioxidants, including resveratrol, the same antioxidant found in red wine and thought to lower the risk of cardiovascular disease—although it is found in considerably lesser amounts in peanuts than in red wine. Like other legumes, the peanut is high in plant protein, and is also a good source of vitamins and minerals. It is an exceptionally good source of biotin (see page 40). However, peanuts are also a common food allergen.

Facing page: Gado gado, an Indonesian dish of vegetables and satay sauce made from peanuts.

Fast Fact

Soybeans are high in nutrients and contain estrogen-like compounds. This is beneficial to many, but can also be harmful. So if you have any hormone-related health concerns or sensitivities, you should not consume soy products without first consulting with your doctor.

Soy (*Glycine max*)

Soy provides a complete source of protein because its seeds contain all the essential amino acids, including methionine, which is lacking in most other legumes. Soy comes in several forms.

Soybeans

Soybeans are not generally eaten on their own but are used to make other foods, including tofu, tempeh, and soy milk. Soybeans are sometimes called "meat of the field" or "poor man's meat" because of their high protein content and their relative affordability. They also contain certain

Tempeh made from soybeans.

peptides (amino acid compounds) that are thought to help regulate blood pressure and blood glucose and support the immune system. Additionally, soybeans are a rich source of isoflavones, phytonutrients that have estrogen-like properties. Some doctors and researchers believe these isoflavones may help relieve menopausal symptoms, reduce the risk of osteoporosis, and help lower cholesterol.

Soybeans are also a good source of antioxidants and omega-3 fatty acids. They can be eaten in their natural form (either fresh or dried), but are rarely served that way in the United States. Instead, processed soybeans are eaten in a variety of forms, ranging from the whole-food forms such as

Tofu made from soybeans.

Raw, dried soybeans.

Fast Fact

The nutritional breakdown of soybeans varies depending on variety and growing conditions, but they generally contain 35 to 40 percent protein, 15 to 20 percent fat, about 30 percent carbohydrates, and around 5 percent minerals. The remainder is water.

tofu, tempeh, and *natto*, to more heavily processed soy protein isolates (SPI) and textured vegetable protein (TVP). The whole-food forms provide the most benefits. Using tofu is one of the easiest ways to add a complete protein to vegetarian meals. Generally, firmer tofu is better than soft, as the more firm the tofu, the higher the protein content.

Edamame

Edamame pods are young soybeans, still inside the pod. Unlike mature soybeans, they are soft and edible. The pods are either boiled or steamed, and then salted before eating. The pod itself is not eaten; the beans are popped into the mouth directly from the pod.

Edamame are popular in Japanese cuisine but are actually of Chinese origin.

Used in both China and Japan for thousands of years, they are now widely available in grocery stores across the United States.

Black Soybeans

Black soybeans are fermented and used in Asian cuisine. They should not be confused with the black beans used in South American and Caribbean dishes.

Black soybeans have the highest known levels of anthocyanins in a plant food. These are the same blue-red antioxidant pigments that appear in fruits and vegetables such as beets, raspberries, and purple corn. They are thought to support heart health.

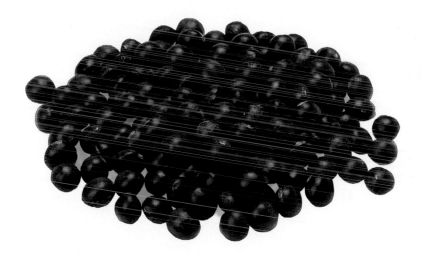

Allergic Reactions

A major concern with soybeans and peanuts is that they can be significant allergens. Reactions range from mild rashes and hives to potentially fatal anaphylaxis, during which swelling of the tongue and throat obstructs or prevents breathing. Although soy and peanuts are safe for most people, it's important to know of any sensitivities before eating them.

Tamarind (*Tamarindus indica*)

The tamarind tree is native to Africa, but it is grown elsewhere around the world for ornamental purposes and for its edible fruit. Tamarind is a legume that bears seed-carrying pods, but neither the big, brown pods nor the beans within are eaten. Instead, people value the greenish pulp inside the pods, which dries to a sticky brown paste that has a sweet-and-sour flavor and works well in sweet desserts, marinades, soups, and stews. Tamarind lacks the high protein content of other beans, largely because people don't eat its seeds (where most of the nutrients are). Nonetheless, the pulp is a good source of fiber and various nutrients, including thiamin, iron, magnesium, and antioxidants. Tamarind is also sometimes used in Eastern medicine.

Fast Fact

Tamarind contains high amounts of tartaric acid, which is a powerful antioxidant that helps neutralize the harmful free radicals in our bodies. Tartaric acid also gives a sour taste to food and is sometimes used to temper overly sweet flavors.

Below: Shrimp served in a tamarind sauce.

Meal Plans

The following meal plans are in accordance with the USDA's dietary guidelines. The needs of individuals will vary, however, so you may need to adjust the plans to suit your specific requirements. If weight loss is not your goal, be guided by your hunger and, as always, please consult with your health practitioner if you have specific dietary or medical needs.

Daily Calorie Requirements

The following meal plans provide approximately 2,000 calories each day. This will meet the needs of a moderately active female who is age fourteen or older.

A moderately active male from age fourteen into adulthood will require approximately 2,400–2,800 calories each day. This can be achieved by increasing quantities by between 20 and 40 percent. Alternatively, eating the following additional foods each day will provide approximately 600 calories:

- 2 slices whole-grain bread
- ½ avocado
- 1½ oz reduced-fat cheese
- 1 cup mixed lettuce, cucumber, and tomato
- 2 small pieces of fresh fruit
- 1 cup low-fat natural yogurt

Quantities may be adjusted according to your specific requirements. If weight loss is not your goal, let your appetite be your guide. Always drink plenty of water to stay hydrated.

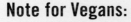

Note for Vegans:

Replace cow's milk, yogurt, and cheese with calcium-fortified soy milk, soy yogurt, and soy cheese throughout these meal plans. Reduced-fat varieties may be used if desired.

Vegetarian and Vegan

The vegetarian meals in this seven-day meal plan are also suitable for vegans unless a vegan alternative is provided.

Seven-Day Meal Plan

Day 1

Vegetarian Breakfast

- 2 slices whole-grain toast topped with ¼ cup low-fat ricotta cheese, 2 tsp. 100% fruit jam, and 1 small sliced pear
- 1 skim milk café latte

Vegan Breakfast

- 2 slices whole-grain toast topped with 1 tbsp. nut spread and 1 sliced banana
- 1 reduced-fat soy café latte

Lunch

- Quinoa with Chickpeas and Mango (p. 305)

Dinner

- Pasta with Pesto and Peas (p. 303)

Snacks

- 1 cup low-fat natural yogurt topped with 1 tbsp. linseed, sunflower, almond (LSA) mix
- 1 cup strawberries
- 1 apple

Day 2

Breakfast

- Muesli with Peanuts, Oats, Dried Fruit, and Seeds (p. 302), served with ½ cup skim milk and 1 cup berries
- 1 skim milk café latte

Lunch

- Sandwich made with 2 slices whole-grain bread, 2 tbsp. hummus (p. 300), 1 small grated carrot, 1 sliced tomato, ½ cup mixed lettuce leaves, and cracked black pepper
- 1 cup low-fat natural yogurt

Vegetarian Dinner

- Corn and Quinoa Fritters (p. 300), served with ½ avocado, 2 tbsp. tomato salsa or relish, and 2 cups mixed lettuce leaves

Vegan Dinner

- Roast Vegetable and Quinoa Salad (p. 303)

Snacks

- 1 apple
- 4 whole-grain crackers with 3 tbsp. reduced-fat cheese and 1 sliced cucumber
- Small handful of mixed raw nuts

Day 3

Breakfast
- Breakfast Smoothie (p. 299)

Lunch
- 4 multigrain crackers topped with 4 tbsp. Baba Ganoush (p. 298), 2 tbsp. pine nuts, and 1 cup arugula
- 1 apple
- 1 cup low-fat natural yogurt

Dinner
- Carrot and Lentil Soup (p. 299) topped with 2 tbsp. lightly toasted pumpkin and sunflower seeds
- 2 slices toasted whole-grain bread rubbed with a fresh garlic clove and topped with 2 thickly sliced ripe tomatoes

Snacks
- 3 tbsp. hummus (p. 300) with 3 cups cut, raw vegetables (try celery, mushrooms, and broccoli)

Day 4

Breakfast
- 2 slices toasted whole-grain bread topped with 1 tbsp. nut spread and 1 sliced banana
- 1 skim milk café latte

Lunch
- 2 Vegetarian "Sushi" Handrolls (p. 308)
- 1 apple

Dinner
- Pumpkin and Chickpea Curry (p. 304), served with 1 cup cooked brown rice (made according to package instructions) and 1 cup steamed green beans

Snacks
- 1 cup low-fat natural yogurt with 1 tbsp. linseed, sunflower, almond (LSA) mix
- Small handful of almonds and cashews

Muesli.

Day 5

Breakfast
- Muesli with Peanuts, Oats, Dried Fruit, and Seeds (p. 302), served with ½ cup skim milk, 2 cups berries, and 1 tbsp. linseed, sunflower, almond (LSA) mix
- 1 skim milk café latte

Lunch
- Sandwich made with 2 slices whole-grain bread, 2 tbsp. hummus (p 300), ½ avocado, 1 sliced tomato, and a few fresh basil leaves
- 1 apple
- 1 skim milk café latte

Vegetarian Dinner
- Sweet Potato Frittata (p. 307), served with 2 cups mixed lettuce, 1 cup cherry tomatoes, 10 walnut halves, and 1 tsp. each of olive oil and balsamic vinegar

Vegan Dinner
- Sweet Potato with Barley and Lentils (p. 307), served with 2 cups mixed lettuce, 1 cup cherry tomatoes, 10 walnut halves, and 1 tsp. each of olive oil and balsamic vinegar

Vegetarian Snacks
- 1 cup low-fat natural yogurt
- 4 whole-grain crackers with 3 tbsp. reduced-fat cheese and a sliced cucumber

Vegan Snacks
- 1 cup soy yogurt
- 2 whole-grain crackers topped with a thickly sliced tomato
- 2 tbsp. Baba Ganoush (p. 298) with 1 cup carrot sticks

Day 6

Vegetarian Breakfast

- 2 eggs cooked in a nonstick frying pan with 1 tsp. olive oil
- 1 cup button mushrooms cooked in a nonstick frying pan with 1 tsp. olive oil
- 2 slices whole-grain toast with 2 tbsp avocado

Vegan Breakfast

- ½ cup baked beans in tomato sauce
- 1 cup button mushrooms cooked in a nonstick frying pan with 1 tsp. olive oil
- 2 slices toasted whole-grain bread with ½ avocado

Lunch

- Sweet Freekeh Salad (p. 306)
- 1 apple

Dinner

- Bean Burritos (p. 298)

Snacks

- 1 cup low-fat natural or soy yogurt
- 1 cup skim milk or soy milk
- 1 pear

Day 7

Breakfast

- Hot Cereal with White Chia and Berries (p. 303)
- 1 cup freshly squeezed orange juice

Vegetarian Lunch

- Sweet Onion and Bell Pepper Omelet (p. 307)
- 1 cup mixed lettuce, 1 sliced pear, and 1 tbsp. shaved Parmesan cheese drizzled with balsamic vinegar

Vegan Lunch

- Bell Pepper and Cannellini Bean Wraps (p. 299)
- 1 pear

Dinner

- Stir-Fry with Tofu and Cashews (p. 306)

Snacks

- 1 cup low-fat natural yogurt
- 1 banana
- 1 skim milk café latte

Gluten-Free

Seven-Day Meal Plan

Day 1

Breakfast
* 1 cup low-fat natural yogurt topped with 1 peeled and chopped kiwifruit, ½ cup raspberries, 1 small sliced banana, 1 tbsp. chia seeds, 10 raw cashews, and 2 tsp. honey

Lunch
* Puy Lentils with Brown Rice and Cherry Tomatoes (p. 304)
* 1 cup freshly squeezed orange juice

Dinner
* Potato Frittata (p. 307)
* 2 cups mixed lettuce leaves
* 1 sliced pear and 1 tbsp shaved Parmesan cheese drizzled with 1 tsp. each of olive oil and balsamic vinegar

Snacks
* 1 skim milk café latte
* 1 tbsp. pumpkin seeds

Day 2

Breakfast
* 2 slices whole grain gluten-free toast topped with ¼ cup reduced-fat ricotta cheese, 1 tbsp. 100% fruit jam, and 1 fresh sliced peach
* 1 skim milk café latte

Lunch
* Corn Wraps with Grated Carrot, Cream Cheese, and Currants (p. 300)

Dinner
* Roast Pumpkin, Beetroot, and Chickpeas (p. 305)

Snacks
* 1 cup low-fat natural yogurt
* ⅓ cup Baba Ganoush (p. 298), served with 2 cups raw, cut vegetables (try mushrooms and cauliflower)
* 1 apple

Day 3

Breakfast
- Quinoa Hot Cereal with Maple Syrup and Berries (p. 305)
- 1 skim milk café latte

Lunch
- Hummus (p. 300) with vegetable sticks
- 3 rice cakes topped with a total of 3 tbsp. nut spread and 1 sliced banana

Dinner
- Kidney Bean Bolognese (p. 301), served with 3 oz. fettuccine cooked according to package instructions and 1 tbsp. shaved Parmesan cheese
- 1 cup steamed fresh green beans topped with 1 tsp. lightly toasted sesame seeds

Snacks
- 1 cup low-fat natural yogurt
- 3 gluten-free crackers topped with a total of 3 tbsp. reduced-fat cheese

Day 4

Breakfast
- 2 slices whole-grain gluten-free toast topped with ¼ cup reduced-fat ricotta cheese, 2 tsp. honey, and 1 sliced banana
- 1 skim milk café latte

Lunch
- Wild Rice with Chickpeas, Raisins, and Herbs (p. 309)
- 1 cup berries

Dinner
- Lentil Soup (p. 302)
- 1 slice toasted whole-grain gluten-free bread topped with ½ avocado and 1 sliced tomato

Snacks
- 1 cup low-fat natural yogurt with 1 tbsp. linseed, sunflower, almond (LSA) mix
- 2 cups carrot sticks and cucumber slices

Whole-grain sandwich with avocado, cheese, tomato, lettuce, and alfalfa.

Day 5

Breakfast

- Pink Smoothie (p. 303)
- 1 apple

Lunch

- Sandwich with 2 slices whole-grain gluten-free bread, 3 tbsp. reduced-fat cheese, ½ avocado, 1 sliced tomato, a small amount of lettuce, and a small handful of alfalfa sprouts

Dinner

- Stir-Fry with Edamame and Mung Beans (p. 306)

Snacks

- 3 gluten-free crackers served with ⅓ cup Baba Ganoush (p. 298)
- 1 oz. dark chocolate
- 2 tbsp. currants

Day 6

Breakfast

- Spinach and Mushroom Omelet (p. 307), served with 1 sliced tomato and ½ avocado
- 1 cup fresh orange juice

Lunch

- Falafel Wrap (p. 300)
- 1 skim milk café latte

Dinner

- Honey-Roasted Pumpkin Risotto (p. 301)

Snacks

- ⅔ cup low-fat natural yogurt
- 1 banana
- 1 apple

Day 7

Breakfast
- Bircher Muesli with Grated Apple and Almonds (p. 299)
- 1 cup strawberries

Lunch
- Vietnamese Rice Noodle Salad (p. 309)
- 1 cup low-fat natural yogurt

Dinner
- Parsnip-Topped Lentil Pie (p. 302)
- 1 cup broccoli and 1 cup snow peas, steamed and topped with
  1 tbsp. slivered almonds

Snacks
- 1 skim milk café latte
- 1 tbsp. pumpkin seeds
- 1 tbsp. sunflower seeds
- 1 cup freshly squeezed orange juice

Vietnamese Rice Noodle Salad.

Recipes

All meal-plan recipes are provided in the following pages.

A Few Important Notes

Servings: Each recipe makes one serving unless otherwise specified.

Storage Life: Each dish should be eaten freshly prepared, unless otherwise stated. Where appropriate, storage guidelines are provided.

To Peel or Not to Peel: All vegetables should be washed but not peeled, unless otherwise stated or preferred. Unpeeled vegetables have a higher dietary fiber content.

A Note on Oats: Oats include a type of gluten known as avenin. Therefore, even oats labeled as "gluten-free" do contain some gluten, though it is a different type than what is found in wheat. For this reason, recipes in this book that contain oats are not considered gluten-free. It is possible that the gluten found in oats is more easily tolerated by some people than other forms of gluten, but this depends on individual sensitivity. The Celiac Disease Foundation states that up to ½ cup of oats can be consumed each day by most people with celiac disease. If you are sensitive to gluten, limit your consumption of oats, or eliminate them entirely from your diet if you experience an adverse reaction.

A Bit About Nuts: Many nuts, even those sold as "raw," have been treated in some way to remove toxins. Completely raw, untreated nuts are not suitable for consumption and can be highly toxic. When purchasing nuts, choose high-quality, unsalted, unroasted varieties.

Recipe Codes

v—suitable for vegetarians

vg—suitable for vegans

gf—suitable for those on gluten-free diets

Baba Ganoush
v | vg | gf

* Makes approximately 1 cup
1 large eggplant
1 garlic clove, peeled
pinch of ground cumin
2 tsp. olive oil
squeeze of fresh lemon juice
fresh cilantro to taste

Bake the whole eggplant at 400°F until the skin is black and charred (approximately 50 minutes), then allow to cool. Remove and discard the skin, then place the baked flesh and the other ingredients in a blender and whiz until smooth. Refrigerate and serve.

Basil Pesto
v | vg | gf

* Makes approximately ⅔ cup
1 clove garlic, peeled
⅓ cup cashew nuts
½ bunch basil, leaves only
¼ cup olive oil

Combine garlic, cashews, and basil in a small food processor and whiz until finely chopped. Stir in olive oil, and refrigerate until ready to serve. Cover any remaining pesto and store in fridge. Use within 2–3 days.

Variation:

—**Arugula Pesto:** Replace half of the basil with arugula and replace cashews with pine nuts. **v | vg | gf**

Basil pesto

Bean Burritos
v

¼ onion, finely chopped
¼ red bell pepper, finely chopped
1 clove garlic, finely chopped
¼ tsp. each cumin, coriander, turmeric
½ red chili, deseeded and finely chopped
½ can diced tomatoes
½ cup water
½ cup cooked red kidney beans (canned or home-prepared), rinsed
2 whole-wheat flour tortillas
1 cup mixed lettuce leaves
1 chopped tomato
1½ tbsp. grated cheddar cheese
1 tbsp. tomato salsa

Spray a nonstick frying pan with a little olive oil, and sauté onion and bell pepper over medium heat until soft. Add garlic, spices, and chili, and cook for another minute. Add tomatoes and water, and increase heat until mixture begins to bubble. Stir in the kidney beans, and simmer uncovered for 30 minutes. Warm the tortillas. Layer bean mixture, lettuce, tomato, cheese, and salsa into tortillas and serve.

Vegan Option:

—Replace cheddar cheese with 1½ tbsp. grated soy cheese. **v | vg**

Bell Pepper and Cannellini Bean Wraps v | vg

2 tsp. olive oil
½ red onion, finely sliced
½ red bell pepper, finely sliced
⅓ cup cooked cannellini beans (canned or
    home-prepared), rinsed
1 cup mixed lettuce
3 whole-grain wraps

Sauté onion and bell pepper in olive oil until soft, then add the cannellini beans. Cook until warmed through. Serve with mixed lettuce in the whole-grain wraps.

Bircher Muesli with Grated Apple and Almonds v | gf

⅓ cup gluten-free rice flakes
½ cup low-fat natural yogurt
2 tbsp. currants
1 apple, peeled and grated
1 tbsp. slivered almonds
a splash of milk

Combine rice flakes, currants, and yogurt and refrigerate overnight. Just before serving, stir in grated apple, almonds, and a little milk. Serve cold.

Breakfast Smoothie v

1 cup skim milk
2 small bananas
1 raw egg
2 tsp. honey
⅓ cup low-fat natural yogurt
2 tbsp. oatmeal
1 tbsp. linseed, sunflower, almond (LSA) mix
pinch of cinnamon

Combine all ingredients in a blender with a few ice cubes and serve.

Note: To avoid the risk of salmonella, use pasteurized eggs, which are now becoming widely available. The pasteurization process kills any harmful bacteria in the egg.

Vegan Option:
—Replace milk and yogurt with soy varieties, replace egg with an extra 1 tbsp. of LSA, and replace honey with maple syrup.

Carrot and Lentil Soup v | vg | gf

* Makes 2 servings
1 small onion, finely chopped
1 small leek, finely sliced
1 clove garlic, peeled and finely chopped
½ cup dry red lentils, rinsed
2 large carrots, grated
2 cups reduced-sodium vegetable stock
1 cup spinach leaves

Spray a heavy saucepan with olive oil, and sauté onion and leek over medium heat until soft. Add garlic and cook for another minute. Add lentils, grated carrot, and stock, and bring to a boil. Reduce to a simmer and cook for 30 minutes. Stir in spinach and remove from heat. Garnish with herbs or toasted seeds.

Corn and Quinoa Fritters   v

¼ cup reduced-fat ricotta cheese
1 egg
2 tbsp low-fat milk
1 tbsp. self-rising whole-wheat flour
2 tbsp. quinoa flakes
1 fresh raw corn cob, kernels only
1 spring onion, finely sliced
¼ red bell pepper, finely chopped
olive oil spray

Beat ricotta, egg, and milk in a bowl until smooth. Add flour, quinoa, corn, onion, and bell pepper. Stir to combine. Spray a non-stick frying pan with olive oil. Cook fritter mixture in balls of 1 tablespoon each for 3–4 minutes on each side, then serve.

Corn Wraps with Grated Carrot, Cream Cheese, and Currants   v | gf

3 gluten-free corn wraps
3 tbsp. reduced-fat cream cheese
2 carrots, peeled and grated
2 tbsp. currants

Layer cream cheese, carrots, and currants evenly into each wrap. Roll and serve.

Falafel Wrap   v | vg | gf

4 gluten-free corn wraps
4 falafel patties (made from falafel mix)
4 tbsp. hummus (recipe below)
2 cups mixed lettuce leaves
1 sliced cucumber

Make the falafel patties according to package instructions, then halve or thickly slice the falafels into smaller pieces. Fill the wraps with the falafels, hummus, lettuce leaves, and cucumber, then serve.

Hummus   v | vg | gf

* Makes approximately 1½ cups
1¼ cup cooked chickpeas (canned or
   home-prepared), rinsed
2 tbsp. tahini
1 clove garlic
squeeze of fresh lemon juice
2 tsp. olive oil
2 tbsp. water

Combine all ingredients in a food processor. Whiz until smooth, adding more water if needed. Cover any remaining hummus and store in fridge. Use within 2–3 days.

Falafels.

Honey Roasted Pumpkin Risotto.

Honey Roasted Pumpkin Risotto   v | gf

* Makes 2 servings
½ cup cubed pumpkin
4 tsp. olive oil
2 tsp. honey
½ onion, finely chopped
½ leek, finely sliced
2 celery stalks, finely chopped
1 small carrot, finely chopped
¾ cup arborio rice
2 cups reduced-sodium vegetable stock
1½ tbsp. grated Parmesan cheese
a handful of fresh parsley, roughly chopped

Place pumpkin in a baking tray with 2 tsp. olive oil and cook at 350°F for 15 minutes. Remove from oven carefully, stir in honey, and return to oven to cook for another 10–15 minutes. Meanwhile, heat 2 tsp. olive oil in a saucepan with lid, and sauté onion, leek, celery, and carrot until soft. Add arborio rice, stir for a minute, pour in stock, and simmer for 18 minutes with the lid on. Remove from heat and stir in Parmesan cheese, pumpkin, and parsley. Allow to sit for a few minutes before serving.

Kidney Bean Bolognese   v | vg | gf

* Makes 2 servings
2 tsp. olive oil
1 small onion, finely chopped
½ red bell pepper, finely chopped
1 clove garlic, finely chopped
1 cup mushrooms, thickly sliced
½ tsp sweet paprika
½ tsp. gluten-free Worcestershire sauce
1¾ cups canned crushed tomatoes
½ cup red wine
½ cup water
1 cup cooked kidney beans (canned or
   home-prepared), rinsed
a handful of fresh parsley, roughly chopped

In a medium saucepan, cook onion and bell pepper in olive oil until soft and beginning to go brown and sticky. Add garlic and mushrooms and cook for another 2–3 minutes. Stir in paprika and Worcestershire sauce, then add tomatoes. Cook for a minute or two before adding red wine, water, and kidney beans. Simmer for 35 minutes, uncovered, adding a little more water if needed. Add parsley and continue to simmer for another 10 minutes. Serve with gluten-free pasta.

Lentil Soup

v | vg | gf

* Makes 2 servings
1 cup dried brown lentils, rinsed
½ red bell pepper, finely chopped
1 small carrot, finely chopped
½ small onion, finely chopped
1 clove garlic, finely chopped
¼ cup tomato paste (no added salt)
a pinch each of cumin, coriander, and paprika
2 cups water
a small handful of parsley, finely chopped

Combine all ingredients except the parsley in a saucepan and bring to a boil. Reduce heat, cover, and simmer for 1½ hours, adding more water as needed. Serve topped with parsley.

Muesli with Peanuts, Oats, Dried Fruit, and Seeds

v | vg

* Makes 2 servings
1 cup rolled oats
6 dried apricot halves, chopped
1 tbsp. quinoa flakes
3 dried apple rings, finely sliced
1 tbsp. peanuts
1 tbsp. mixed pumpkin and sunflower seeds
1 pinch of ground cinnamon

Combine all ingredients and store in an airtight container in the pantry, or the fridge in hot weather. If the ingredients are fresh and the muesli is stored correctly, it will keep for several months.

Parsnip-Topped Lentil Pie

v | gf

* Makes 2 servings
½ cup dried red lentils, rinsed
1 tbsp. olive oil
½ small onion, finely chopped
1 clove garlic, finely chopped
½ red bell pepper, finely chopped
2 celery stalks, finely chopped
1 carrot, peeled and finely chopped
1 cup mushrooms, sliced
2 tsp. red wine vinegar
2 tsp. tomato paste
¾ cup canned chopped tomatoes
a sprig each of fresh thyme and rosemary
10 green beans, cut into ½-inch lengths
a handful of fresh parsley

Topping

1 parsnip, peeled and cut into ½-inch cubes
1 potato, peeled and cut into ½-inch cubes
3 tbsp. skim milk
2 tbsp. grated Parmesan cheese
1 tbsp. butter

Preheat oven to 425°F. Simmer lentils in a saucepan of water for 15 minutes until tender. Drain, and reserve 1 cup of the cooking water. Meanwhile, gently cook onion and garlic with oil in a non-stick frying pan for 5–6 minutes until soft. Add bell pepper, celery, carrot, and mushrooms and cook for another 5–6 minutes. Increase heat, add red wine vinegar and tomato paste, and cook for a minute before adding canned tomatoes, thyme, and rosemary. Cook for another minute, then add lentils, reserved liquid, and beans. Simmer for 10 minutes, remove from heat, then stir in parsley. For topping, steam parsnip and potato until tender, then mash with milk, cheese, and butter. Divide lentil mixture between two baking dishes, top with parsnip mash, and bake for 15 minutes until top is golden.

Pasta with Pesto and Peas · v

3 oz. fettuccine pasta
¼ cup fresh green peas
6 small asparagus spears
1 cup broccoli florets
2 tbsp. basil pesto (p. 298)
1 tbsp. shaved Parmesan cheese
1 tsp. sesame seeds, lightly toasted

Cook pasta according to instructions, adding the peas to the cooking water in the last 2 minutes. Meanwhile, steam the asparagus and broccoli for 3–4 minutes. Drain the peas and pasta, stir in the pesto and Parmesan, and season with freshly cracked black pepper. Serve with asparagus and broccoli topped with toasted sesame seeds.

Vegan Option:
—Omit Parmesan cheese and sprinkle pasta with 2 tsp. slivered almonds · **v | vg**

Pink Smoothie · v | gf

1 cup skim milk
2 tbsp. linseed, sunflower, and almond (LSA) mix
1 cup fresh or frozen berries
⅓ cup low-fat berry yogurt
2 tsp. maple syrup

Combine all ingredients in a blender with a few ice cubes and mix until smooth. Serve immediately.

Hot Cereal with White Chia and Berries · v

½ cup rolled oats
¼ cup water
½ cup skim milk
2 tbsp. white chia seeds
1 cup berries

Cook oats and water over low heat in a small saucepan. Stir in milk and continue to cook until it reaches the desired consistency, adding a little more water if needed. Remove from heat and stir in the chia seeds. Pour into a bowl, top with berries, and serve.

Hot Cereal with White Chia and Berries.

303

Pumpkin and Chickpea Curry.

Pumpkin and Chickpea Curry   v | vg | gf

* Makes 2 servings
1 tbsp. olive oil
1 onion, finely chopped
2 garlic cloves, peeled and finely chopped
½ tsp. each of ginger, turmeric, and cinnamon
⅔ cup chopped tomatoes
½ cup red lentils, rinsed
1 cup pumpkin, cubed
2½ cups reduced-sodium vegetable stock
⅔ cup cooked chickpeas (canned or
    home-prepared), rinsed
a handful of fresh cilantro

Sauté onion in oil over medium heat in a heavy-based saucepan until soft. Add garlic and spices and cook for a further minute. Add tomatoes and cook for a further 1–2 minutes, then add lentils, pumpkin, and stock. Simmer for 30 minutes. Add chickpeas and cilantro and simmer for a further 30 minutes.

Puy Lentils with Brown Rice and Cherry Tomatoes   v | vg | gf

½ cup brown rice
⅔ cup cooked puy lentils (equal to ⅓ cup dry
    puy lentils), rinsed
¼ small red onion, finely diced
a handful of fresh parsley, roughly chopped
10 walnut halves, roughly chopped
½ cup cherry tomatoes, halved

Dressing
2 tsp. olive oil
2 tsp. maple syrup
a pinch of ground cumin

Cook the rice according to package instructions. To make the dressing, gently heat dressing ingredients in a small saucepan over low heat until combined, then set aside. Mix the rice and remaining ingredients together in a salad bowl, drizzle the dressing over the top, toss well, and refrigerate until ready to serve.

Quinoa Hot Cereal with Maple Syrup and Berries   v | gf

½ cup quinoa flakes
½ cup water
½ cup skim milk
2 tsp. maple syrup
1 tbsp. slivered almonds
1 cup mixed berries

Cook quinoa flakes with water over low heat until it's the consistency of hot cereal. Add milk and maple syrup and continue to cook for another minute or so. Serve topped with mixed berries and almonds.

Quinoa with Chickpeas and Mango   v | vg | gf

½ cup red quinoa
⅔ cup cooked chickpeas (canned or
   home-prepared), rinsed
1 mango, peeled and cubed
1 cup spinach leaves, roughly chopped
a small handful of almonds, roughly chopped
1 spring onion, finely sliced
squeeze of fresh lime juice
1 tsp. olive oil
a small handful of fresh cilantro

Cook quinoa according to package instructions. When quinoa has cooled, combine with other ingredients and serve.

Roast Pumpkin, Beetroot, and Chickpeas   v | vg | gf

2 raw beets, cut into ½-inch cubes
2 cups pumpkin, cut into ½-inch cubes
1 tbsp. olive oil
⅔ cup cooked chickpeas (canned or home-
   prepared), rinsed
½ tbsp. pine nuts
a small handful of parsley

Steam beets for 8–10 minutes. Mix beets and pumpkin with olive oil and bake at 350°F for 30 minutes. Remove from oven and stir in the chickpeas, pine nuts, and parsley, then season with freshly cracked black pepper. Serve warm or at room temperature.

Roast Vegetable and Quinoa Salad   v | vg

½ cup quinoa
1 small zucchini, roughly chopped
1 red bell pepper, roughly chopped
1 small eggplant, thickly sliced
½ red onion, cut into wedges
1 tsp. olive oil
⅔ cup cooked chickpeas (canned or
   home-prepared), rinsed
1 tbsp pine nuts
2 cups baby spinach leaves
2 tbsp. tomato chutney
1 tbsp. avocado, peeled and diced

Cook quinoa according to package instructions. Meanwhile, toss onion, zucchini, bell pepper, and eggplant with olive oil and bake at 350°F for 30 minutes. When cooked, combine vegetables with cooked quinoa, chickpeas, and pine nuts and allow to cool. Toss with baby spinach leaves, top with tomato chutney and avocado, and serve.

Stir-Fry with Tofu and Cashews
v | vg

½ cup brown rice

1 cup broccoli florets

1 cup snow peas

½ cup sliced carrot

½ cup yellow bell pepper strips

½ cup sliced zucchini

a small handful of cashew nuts

1 garlic clove, peeled and finely sliced

½ inch fresh ginger, grated

1 red chili, deseeded and finely sliced

2 tsp. reduced-sodium soy sauce

2 tsp. black bean paste

1 tsp. sesame oil

1 tbsp. reduced-sodium vegetable stock

¼ cup silken tofu, cubed

a handful of fresh cilantro, chopped

Cook rice according to package instructions and keep warm. Mix together the broccoli, snow peas, carrot, bell pepper, and zucchini in a bowl, and sprinkle with nuts, garlic, ginger, and chili. Drizzle with soy sauce and black bean paste. Heat oil and stock in a wok, add vegetable mixture, and toss for 3–4 minutes over high heat. Add tofu and gently toss until warmed through. Serve with rice, garnished with fresh cilantro.

Gluten-Free Options:

—Replace soy sauce and black bean paste with gluten-free varieties. **v | vg | gf**

—**Stir-Fry with Edamame and Mung Beans:** Replace the tofu with ⅓ cup peeled, fresh edamame beans (or frozen edamame beans). Replace zucchini with ½ cup mung bean sprouts. **v | vg | gf**

Sweet Freekeh Salad
v | vg

½ cup freekeh

½ cup cooked puy or brown lentils (canned or home-prepared), rinsed

¼ small red onion, finely chopped

1 tbsp. currants

1 tbsp. mixed pine nuts and pumpkin seeds

5 almonds, roughly chopped

a handful of fresh parsley, chopped

Dressing

2 tsp maple syrup

1 tsp. olive oil

pinch of ground cumin

Cook the freekeh according to package instructions and allow to cool. To make the dressing, gently heat the dressing ingredients in a small saucepan over low heat until maple syrup melts, then allow to cool. Place remaining ingredients with freekeh in a small bowl, drizzle with dressing, and toss well to combine. Refrigerate until required.

Sweet Onion and Bell Pepper Omelet   v | gf

2 tsp. olive oil
½ red onion, finely sliced
½ red bell pepper, finely sliced
1 small potato, thinly sliced
3 eggs, lightly whisked
handful of fresh parsley

In a nonstick frying pan, sauté onion, bell pepper, and potato in 1 tsp. oil over low heat until soft. Remove from pan and wipe pan clean. Heat remaining oil and add the eggs. Cook over medium heat until almost set. Pile vegetables and parsley on one side of omelet and fold the other side over the top. Cook for another minute or so and serve.

Variation:

—**Spinach and Mushroom Omelet:** Replace potato with ½ cup sliced mushrooms and ½ cup spinach leaves. **v | gf**

Sweet Potato Frittata   v | gf

2 tsp. olive oil
½ onion, finely sliced
½ red bell pepper, finely sliced
½ medium sweet potato, finely sliced
3 eggs, lightly whisked
handful of fresh parsley

Cook onion and bell pepper in 1 tsp. olive oil over low heat in a small ovenproof frying pan until beginning to soften. Add sliced sweet potato and cook with lid on until tender. Remove from pan and wipe clean. Add another 1 tsp olive oil, pour in eggs, and cook until just beginning to set underneath. Add vegetables, press into egg mixture with the parsley, and continue to cook until beginning to brown underneath. Set top under a broiler, then slice and serve.

Variation:

—**Potato Frittata:** Replace sweet potato with 1 medium potato. **v | gf**

Sweet Potato with Barley and Lentils   v | vg

2 tsp. olive oil
½ onion, roughly chopped
½ red bell pepper, roughly chopped
1 cup sweet potato, roughly chopped
¼ cup pearl barley
½ cup cooked brown lentils (canned or home-prepared), rinsed
1 cup lettuce leaves
½ cup cherry tomatoes
1 tsp. balsamic vinegar

Combine 1 tsp. olive oil with the onion, sweet potato, and bell pepper, and roast in a 400°F oven for 30 minutes. Meanwhile, cook the barley according to package instructions. Mix it with the roasted vegetables and the lentils. When completely cool, mix in the lettuce, tomatoes, 1 tsp. olive oil, and balsamic vinegar. Refrigerate until ready to eat.

Vegetarian "Sushi" Handrolls

v | vg

* Makes 1 serving of 2–3 rolls
⅓ cup short-grain brown rice
2 tsp. soy sauce
2 tbsp. rice vinegar
1 tsp. sugar
2 nori sheets
½ cucumber, peeled and cut into
   matchstick-size pieces
½ carrot, peeled and shaved or cut into
   matchstick-size pieces
⅛ avocado, peeled and sliced
   lengthwise
a few slivers of bell pepper (optional)
a few fresh lettuce leaves (optional)
1 tsp. wasabi powder mixed to a paste
   according to package instructions
   (optional)
extra soy sauce (optional)

Cook rice according to the package instructions, adding 1 tsp. soy sauce to the water. Once cooked, transfer the rice to a ceramic bowl. Add remaining soy sauce and sugar to the rice vinegar and stir through the rice. Allow to cool.

Assembling the rolls can be done with a sushi mat, but an easier way is to roll them in your hand. Simply cradle a nori sheet in the palm of your left hand (or right hand, if you are left-handed), rough side facing up. One edge should extend beyond your little finger, and the other three should be within your palm. Place a ½-cup ball of rice on the nori sheet in the center of your palm. Dig a little hole in the rice and fill with the cucumbers, carrots, and avocado, as well as bell pepper and lettuce (if using)—but don't overstuff. Using your other hand, use your thumb to lift the corner of the nori closest to your wrist and fold it over the ingredients to form a cone. Continue rolling the cone to form a tighter roll, using single rice grains as needed to help seal the roll. (This might take some practice!) Serve with wasabi paste and soy sauce for dipping if desired.

Gluten-Free Option:
—Replace soy sauce with gluten-free soy sauce. v | vg | gf

Vegetarian "Sushi" Handrolls.

Vietnamese Rice Noodle Salad

v | vg | gf

3 oz. bean thread noodles

1 medium carrot, peeled and
  coarsely grated

2 celery stalks, finely julienned

1 cup cabbage, finely shredded

1 spring onion, finely sliced

1 red chili, deseeded and finely sliced

Dressing

½ garlic clove, finely chopped

½ inch fresh ginger, finely chopped

1 tsp. each of gluten free soy sauce, rice
  wine vinegar, and lime juice

1 tsp. maple syrup

2 tbsp. peanuts

Prepare noodles according to package instructions. Place noodles, carrot, celery, cabbage, onion, and chili in a salad bowl. In a separate bowl, whisk dressing ingredients together until the maple syrup is dissolved. Drizzle dressing over salad, toss to combine, then serve.

Wild Rice with Chickpeas, Raisins, and Herbs

v | vg | gf

½ cup wild rice

2 tsp. olive oil

½ small onion, finely chopped

½ small fennel bulb, finely chopped

2 stalks celery, finely chopped

a pinch of ground cumin and fennel

⅓ cup cooked chickpeas (canned or home-
  prepared), rinsed

2 tbsp. slivered almonds

1 tbsp. raisins

a squeeze of fresh lemon juice

Cook the rice according to the package instructions. In a nonstick frying pan, cook onion, fennel, and celery in 1 tsp. olive oil over medium heat until just beginning to soften. Stir in cumin and fennel, remove from heat, and combine with rice, chickpeas, almonds, and raisins. Drizzle with re-maining 1 tsp. olive oil and a squeeze of fresh lemon juice, then refrigerate until ready to serve.

Wild Rice with Chickpeas, Raisins, and Herbs.

Glossary

aleuron A protein-rich layer surrounding the seed of cereal grains that, together with the pericarp, forms the bran.

alkaloid A type of chemical, usually toxic, that is derived from plants.

allergens Substances that provoke abnormal immune-system reactions.

amino acids Components of proteins that link together in different configurations to form the physical structures of the body.

amylopectin A type of starch found in grains. It is responsible for the gluelike quality of sticky rices when they are cooked.

amylose Another type of starch found in grains. Unlike amylopectin, it does not form a gel or become sticky upon cooking.

ancient grains Generally refers to the ancient wheats (einkorn, emmer, spelt, and Khorasan) that once fell out of the human diet but are now reemerging.

anemia A condition whereby the blood is unable to transport oxygen sufficiently due to a decreased number of red blood cells.

anthocyanins A group of hundreds of plant pigments found in blue and dark blue-red plants, valued for their antioxidant properties.

antinutrients Plant substances that inhibit the absorption of nutrients and can be damaging to health. Cooking is one way to eliminate them, but some, including phytates and flavonoids, also contain beneficial properties such as antioxidants.

antioxidant A compound that neutralizes unstable and damaging substances in the body that form after exposure to pollutants or as byproducts of the metabolic process.

atherosclerosis A condition whereby the artery walls have thickened as a result of a buildup of fatty materials.

avenin A glutenlike protein found in some grains.

beta-carotene A plant pigment found in yellow, orange, and red fruits and vegetables. It is a precursor to vitamin A and has antioxidant properties.

beta-glucan A type of soluble dietary fiber.

bioavailability Refers to the extent to which ingested micronutrients are available for use by the body.

bracts In cereal grains, the coarse, leaflike structures that form the hull and surround and protect the seed. They are also referred to as glumes.

bran The hard outer layers of cereal grains, including the protein-rich aleuron and the fibrous pericarp. Along with the endosperm and the embryo (or germ), it one of the three main parts of a cereal grain.

Facing page: Pasta with pesto and peas (p. 303).

calorie A unit of measurement that quantifies the amount of energy produced when a particular food is metabolized by the body.

cancer A type of disease caused by the growth of abnormal cells.

carbohydrates One of the three macronutrients (along with fat and protein) that are essential for life. Carbohydrates are the main source of energy for most humans.

carotenoids A group of plant pigments, including beta-carotene, found in yellow, orange, red, and dark green plants. They are valued for their antioxidant properties.

cereal grains The edible seeds of grasses such as wheat, rye, and oats, among others.

chlorophyll The green plant pigment that is essential for photosynthesis, the process by which plants convert light energy into chemical energy.

cholesterol A substance that occurs naturally in the organs and fluids of the body and is also found in some foods, such as egg yolks and butter. There are two types: HDL ("good cholesterol"), considered beneficial, and LDL ("bad cholesterol"), which increases the risk of cardiovascular disease and other serious health problems.

complementary proteins Two types of food proteins, each lacking in certain essential amino acids, paired to create a meal that contains all of them.

complete protein A protein food that contains all of the essential amino acids.

diabetes A health condition in which one's blood sugar levels are too high.

dry beans The edible dry seeds of legumes, also known as pulses.

embryo The part of a seed that grows into a new plant, also referred to as the germ.

endosperm Starchy plant tissue found in the seed of a plant; it nourishes the embryo. Along with the bran and the embryo, the endosperm is one of three main parts of a cereal grain.

enzymes Types of proteins found in all plants and animals that initiate or speed up chemical processes in the body.

essential amino acids Those the body is unable to produce and therefore must ingest.

fats One of three macronutrients (along with proteins and carbohydrates) that are essential for life. Fats pad and help to insulate the body, and are also an important secondary source of energy after carbohydrates.

fermentation A process, facilitated by yeasts, molds, and bacteria that alters the composition of foods, generally to preserve them or make them more digestible.

fiber, dietary The generally indigestible and fibrous component of plant foods that is valued for its ability to add bulk to food and aid its passage through the digestive system.

flavonoids A group of plant substances that have antioxidant and anti-inflammatory properties. They are also considered to be antinutrients because they can inhibit the absorption of other nutrients, especially certain minerals.

free radicals Unstable and damaging substances produced in the body as a result of the metabolic process or after exposure to environmental pollutants.

free-threshing grains These grains are not fully enclosed in an outer hull and can be separated from the hull upon threshing alone; the opposite of hulled grains.

germ Another term for embryo.

gluten A protein found in several cereal grains. Gluten provides dough with its elastic and chewy properties.

glycemic index (GI) A tool that measures the rate at which carbohydrates raise blood sugar levels. Low-GI foods are digested and release energy at a slower, more sustained rate than high-GI foods, helping to keep blood sugar levels more stable.

grain The small, dry, single-seeded fruit of a grass plant. The term is also used to refer to grasses that are grown as food crops, including wheat, rye, corn, and others.

groats The edible whole grain of a cereal grain after the outer hull has been removed.

hull The inedible outer casing of a grain, formed by coarse, leaflike structures known as bracts (or glumes). It is also referred to as the husk.

hulled grain Hulled grains are fully enclosed in a tough outer hull (or husk). They require additional mechanical processing after threshing to release the seed from the hull.

husk Another term for hull.

hybrid A plant created by natural or artificial crossbreeding of two compatible plants.

immune system A system of processes in the body that protects it from disease.

incomplete protein A protein lacking in one or more essential amino acids.

inflammation Part of the body's response to cell damage caused by injury, infection, radiation, toxins, and irritants. It plays a critical role in healing and recovery. Unfortunately, the body's ability to regulate inflammation can be compromised, leading to chronic or prolonged inflammation, which can cause diseases such as rheumatoid arthritis.

insulin A hormone that enables the body to use the energy from food.

isoflavones A group of plant proteins with antioxidant and estrogen-like properties.

lectins Toxic plant substances thought to be part of the plants' survival mechanisms. In plant foods, legumes and grains contain the most lectins, but the levels absorbed are generally insufficient to damage health. Concentrated amounts can cause digestive issues and other health problems. The lethal poison ricin is a lectin of the castor oil plant.

legumes Pod-bearing plants of the botanical family Fabaceae. The pod, or fruit, of these plants has two seams, inside of which are the seeds.

lignans One of the major groups of phytoestrogens (plant estrogens). They also have antioxidant properties.

lignins Not to be confused with lignans, these are plant molecules that help form the cell walls in plants.

limited protein Another term for incomplete protein.

lycopene A powerful antioxidant and one of the many carotenoids.

lysine An essential amino acid. It is generally not in grains, but is plentiful in legumes.

macronutrients Three of the seven types of essential nutrients—carbohydrates, fats, and proteins—that exist in a tangible form and are ingested into the body.

methionine An essential amino acid. It is generally not in legumes (with some exceptions, including soy), but is plentiful in grains.

micronutrients Generally refers to two of the seven types of essential nutrients—vitamins and minerals—that exist in a microscopic form.

minerals Along with vitamins, one of the two categories of essential micronutrients. They form the hard structures of the body, such as teeth and bones, and are also components of various enzymes and other compounds. They include calcium and iron, among others.

nitrogen-fixing In legumes, a term that refers to the ability of legumes to convert nitrogen into a form that is usable by other plants and animals.

nixtamilization A process that converts niacin found in corn into a form that is available to the human body.

nonessential amino acids Amino acids that the body is able to produce.

nutrients These are the ingested substances that support life. Seven are considered essential for life itself: carbohydrates, fats, proteins, vitamins, minerals, fiber, and water.

obesity A condition where high levels of excess body fat have an adverse effect on health. It is a major risk factor for serious health conditions, including cardiovascular disease and some cancers.

osteoporosis A disease caused by calcium loss or deficiency, resulting in weakened bones.

peptides A protein chain formed by two or more linked amino acids.

pericarp One of the outer layers surrounding the endosperm and embryo of cereal grains

phenolic acids Aromatic plant compounds that have antioxidant properties.

phytates Substances found in seeds that have antioxidant properties, but are also considered antinutrients because they inhibit the absorption of some other nutrients.

phytoestrogen A form of estrogen found in some plants.

phytonutrients Nutrients found in plants; also referred to as plant nutrients. Phytonutrients are undergoing extensive research and are not yet classified as essential.

plant sterols Also known as phytosterols, these plant compounds inhibit the body's absorption of cholesterol and can be effective in lowering LDL ("bad") cholesterol.

polyphenol A generic term for the thousands of plant compounds that have antioxidant properties, including lignans, flavonoids, phenolic acids, and stilbenes.

proteins One of the three macronutrients (along with carbohydrates and fats) that are ingested and are essential for sustaining life. Proteins form the physical structures of the body and are also essential for growth and other processes within the body.

pseudograins Plants that have similar qualities to cereal grains, but their fruits bear more than one seed. In contrast, the fruits of cereal grains are single-seeded.

pulses The edible dry seeds of legumes. They are also known as dry beans.

refined flour The endosperm of a cereal grain, with the embryo (germ) and husk removed. Refined flour is less nutritious than whole-grain flour.

resveratrol Part of the stilbene group of polyphenols, resveratrol is found in peanuts, as well as in red grapes, berries, and other plant foods.

rhizobia Soil bacteria within the roots of legumes that fixes nitrogen (*see* nitrogen-fixing).

saponins A group of plant compounds that have distinctive foaming and soaplike qualities. They are considered antinutrients, and some are toxic. Conversely, some offer antioxidants and other health benefits. They are found in many legumes, some pseudograins (including quinoa), and in other vegetables. Quinoa is generally washed prior to cooking to remove the saponins.

satiety The feeling of being full after eating.

stilbene A category of polyphenols.

vegan diet A strict vegetarian diet that excludes all animal products, including dairy foods and honey.

vegetarian diet A diet that excludes meat, but generally not other animal products such as milk, cheese, eggs, and honey.

vitamins Along with minerals, vitamins are one of the two categories of essential micro-nutrients. Most cannot be produced in the body and must be ingested. They play a critical role in the body's chemical processes.

water Made up of hydrogen and oxygen, water is present in every cell of the body and plays a vital role in all of its processes. The human body is approximately 66 percent water.

whole grain A grain, or a grain food, that contains all three nutritional components: the endosperm, bran, and embryo (or germ). It does not include the inedible hull.

xeaxanthine A carotenoid that is considered especially beneficial to eye health.

Index

ACKNOWLEDGMENTS AND CREDITS

Acknowledgments

The publisher and author thank Danielle Bowman and Karen Inge for their valuable contributions to this project.

Credits

Credits are listed by page. Multiple credits per page are listed in a clockwise sequence.